U.S. Department of Defense Civilian Casualty Policies and Procedures

An Independent Assessment

MICHAEL J. MCNERNEY, GABRIELLE TARINI, KAREN M. SUDKAMP,
LARRY LEWIS, MICHELLE GRISÉ, PAULINE MOORE

Prepared for the Office of the Secretary of Defense

NATIONAL DEFENSE RESEARCH INSTITUTE

For more information on this publication, visit **www.rand.org/t/RRA418-1**.

About RAND

The RAND Corporation is a research organization that develops solutions to public policy challenges to help make communities throughout the world safer and more secure, healthier and more prosperous. RAND is nonprofit, nonpartisan, and committed to the public interest. To learn more about RAND, visit www.rand.org.

Research Integrity

Our mission to help improve policy and decisionmaking through research and analysis is enabled through our core values of quality and objectivity and our unwavering commitment to the highest level of integrity and ethical behavior. To help ensure our research and analysis are rigorous, objective, and nonpartisan, we subject our research publications to a robust and exacting quality-assurance process; avoid both the appearance and reality of financial and other conflicts of interest through staff training, project screening, and a policy of mandatory disclosure; and pursue transparency in our research engagements through our commitment to the open publication of our research findings and recommendations, disclosure of the source of funding of published research, and policies to ensure intellectual independence. For more information, visit www.rand.org/about/principles.

RAND's publications do not necessarily reflect the opinions of its research clients and sponsors.

Published by the RAND Corporation, Santa Monica, Calif.
© 2022 RAND Corporation
RAND® is a registered trademark.

Library of Congress Cataloging-in-Publication Data is available for this publication.

ISBN: 978-1-9774-0699-6

Cover image: Erik De Castro/Alamy Stock Photo.

About This Report

Section 1721 of the Fiscal Year 2020 National Defense Authorization Act requires that a federally funded research and development center conduct an independent assessment of U.S. Department of Defense standards, processes, procedures, and policy relating to civilian casualties resulting from U.S. military operations. The Office of the Under Secretary of Defense for Policy requested that the RAND Corporation undertake this assessment, and RAND researchers worked in collaboration with those from CNA. This report should be of interest to members of Congress and congressional staff, as well as Department of Defense and other U.S. government officials, U.S. and partner military personnel, and United Nations and nongovernmental organization officials.

National Security Research Division

The research reported here was completed in February 2021 and underwent security review with the sponsor and the Defense Office of Prepublication and Security Review before public release.

This research was sponsored by the Office of the Secretary of Defense and conducted within the International Security and Defense Policy Center of the RAND National Security Research Division (NSRD), which operates the National Defense Research Institute (NDRI), a federally funded research and development center sponsored by the Office of the Secretary of Defense, the Joint Staff, the Unified Combatant Commands, the Navy, the Marine Corps, the defense agencies, and the defense intelligence enterprise.

For more information on the RAND International Security and Defense Policy Center, see www.rand.org/nsrd/isdp or contact the director (contact information is provided on the webpage).

Acknowledgments

We greatly appreciate the assistance provided by Deputy Assistant Secretary of Defense for Stability and Humanitarian Affairs Stephanie Hammond, as well as her staff, particularly Cara Negrette, Anna Williams, and David Cate. We are also grateful to Lt Col Breanna Fulton, Lt Col Mark Cramer, and Loren Voss for their frequent support. Thanks to Jenny McAvoy from InterAction for helping facilitate numerous fruitful discussions with nongovernmental organization officials and to Dan Mahanty from the Center for Civilians in Conflict for his assistance and insights.

We are indebted to our reviewers, Brig Gen (ret.) Matthew C. Isler and Shelly Culbertson, whose feedback improved this report tremendously.

We also recognize the invaluable contributions of the dozens of leaders and experts whom we interviewed from across the Department of Defense, Department of State, and many nongovernmental organizations.

Summary

Section 1721 of the Fiscal Year 2020 National Defense Authorization Act required that a federally funded research and development center conduct an independent assessment of U.S. Department of Defense (DoD) standards, processes, procedures, and policy relating to civilian casualties resulting from U.S. military operations. Using the guidelines of Section 1721 as a foundation, the RAND Corporation, in collaboration with CNA, organized a team to conduct research on the following four dimensions:

1. assessments of civilian harm
2. investigations of civilian harm
3. responses to civilian harm
4. DoD resourcing and structure to address civilian harm.[1]

This report describes our findings and recommendations based on this research.

From its most-senior leaders to military operators in the field, DoD has expressed a strong commitment to complying with the law of war and to mitigating civilian harm for legal, moral, and strategic reasons and for ensuring mission-effectiveness. DoD and each of its military services have detailed manuals on the law of war. But above and beyond its law of war obligations, DoD implements policies and procedures at multiple levels to mitigate civilian harm during armed conflict. The combatant commands follow DoD-wide and theater-specific rules of engagement, which set forth the circumstances in which force may be used, as well as the limitations on its use. The importance of civilian protection is emphasized in U.S. military training at every level—including basic training, professional military education, and pre-deployment training.

DoD's efforts to understand and account for civilian harm after it has occurred are sometimes viewed as secondary to efforts to mitigate the risks of civilian harm in the first place. As we discuss throughout this report, however, there are important reasons to focus on improving DoD's post-strike assessments, investigations, and responses alongside pre-strike mitigation.

---

[1] In this report, we often use the term *civilian harm*, which we define broadly to include damage, injury, or death that adversely affects civilian populations, structures, or infrastructure as a consequence of military operations.

For example, **assessments** of civilian harm enable operational learning within the force and support feedback loops that can reduce the risk of future incidents and improve mission-effectiveness. They demonstrate accountability and transparency and give the U.S. government and public a better ability to consider the costs of war. Assessments are part of the United States' commitment to monitor its compliance with the law of war and go beyond those standards to mitigate civilian harm in future operations.

Whereas DoD performs assessments that focus primarily on determining whether civilian harm has occurred as a result of U.S. military operations, DoD may direct more-extensive **investigations** to obtain additional facts or details about a civilian-harm incident. In short, assessments tell us what happened, and investigations can tell us why. Uncovering the latter information—that is, identifying the causal factors of civilian harm—is critical in order for DoD to learn from mistakes and improve its capacity to mitigate civilian harm in the future. Investigations, if done properly, can strengthen the learning process begun by a civilian-harm assessment and can help the military institutionalize hard-earned lessons.

Responses to civilian-harm incidents can take many forms, including the provision of *ex gratia* payments to the affected community and individuals.[2] Such responses provide assistance to those affected by the tragedy of war, advance the U.S. mission on the ground, build rapport with local communities, and reinforce the U.S. relationship with the host-nation government.

To pursue this research and meet the requirements of Congress, we analyzed a wide variety of U.S. government documents, government and nongovernmental reports and articles, battle histories, and operational after-action reports. We interviewed more than 80 DoD and State Department officials, military planners and operators, members of civilian casualty cells (CIVCAS cells), and personnel from nongovernmental organizations (NGOs). We also collected CIVCAS credibility assessment reports (CCARs), civilian casualty allegation closure reports, documentation from commander-directed investigations, and military strike data for deeper analysis. Where possible, we built on the research of past studies, particularly the 2018 Civilian Casualty Review commissioned by the Chairman of the Joint Chiefs of Staff.[3] For most of our interviews, we focused on DoD's present-day policies and procedures. Where possible, we leveraged interviewees' experiences in Afghanistan, Iraq, and Syria, where most U.S.-caused civilian casualties have occurred in recent years. We also interviewed personnel with knowledge of civilian-harm issues in U.S. military operations in Africa.

Our discussions with NGO personnel and the data they provided were important to our research. Many NGOs work to document civilian harm in conflict zones

---

[2]   DoD's provision of condolences is made *ex gratia*—that is, without DoD recognizing any legal obligation to provide the assistance.

[3]   Joint Staff, *Civilian Casualty (CIVCAS) Review*, Washington, D.C., April 17, 2018.

and advocate for greater civilian protection in U.S. military operations. The 2018 Joint Staff review found that reports of civilian casualties from external sources constituted 58 percent of the total number of civilian casualties that DoD identified from 2015 to 2017.[4] Estimates of civilian casualties from NGOs and other external sources have often been far higher than estimates from DoD assessments, which has been a challenge to DoD's credibility and has drawn attention from Congress, the media, and senior officials. DoD's continuous improvement in the realm of civilian-harm mitigation is bolstered by the work of NGOs and other external sources of information. NGOs are also important because they can challenge DoD assumptions and prompt reexamination and reflection.

Cross-Cutting Insights

In the next section, we discuss our full range of findings and recommendations. Here, we provide insights that cut across the study's four lines of research, built on the evidence we collected.

First, DoD has built a strong foundation for compliance with the law of war, including the protection of civilians, during armed conflict. The *Department of Defense Law of War Manual* consolidates a vast array of existing legal guidance, making legal information available in an organized and centralized way to U.S. commanders, legal practitioners, and other DoD personnel responsible for implementing the law of war during military operations.[5] A commitment to those obligations was evident in our conversations with DoD personnel, from senior officials to military planners and operators in the field. Moreover, as a matter of policy, the U.S. military often conducts its operations under policy standards and procedures that exceed the requirements of the law of war.[6] And although we found gaps and inconsistencies in guidance, DoD has committed to an extensive array of civilian-harm policies, standards, processes, and procedures.

---

[4] Joint Staff, 2018, p. 11.

[5] Office of the General Counsel, U.S. Department of Defense, *Department of Defense Law of War Manual,* Washington, D.C.: U.S. Department of Defense, Washington, D.C.: U.S. Department of Defense, December 2016. The manual identifies the following principles as foundational to the law of war: military necessity, humanity, proportionality (economy of force), distinction (between civilians and combatants), and honor. It characterizes the protection of civilians as one of the main purposes of the law of war. The manual explains that the law of war imposes both negative duties (requiring that military forces refrain from directing military operations against civilians) and affirmative duties (requiring that military forces take precautions to protect civilians) and then explains in detail the content of those duties.

[6] DoD generally uses the terms *law of war* and *law of armed conflict* interchangeably. According to the DoD's law of war manual, both terms are used in DoD directives and training materials. International organizations and NGOs also use the term *international humanitarian law* (Office of the General Counsel, U.S. Department of Defense, 2016, p. 8).

Second, we found that DoD's current approach to assessing, investigating, and responding to civilian harm has considerable weaknesses in key areas and is inconsistent across theaters. Although it is important for commands to have the flexibility to tailor their responses to particular regions and circumstances, the lack of a clear baseline of standardized DoD guidance and requirements creates challenges and confusion. We found encouraging signs of DoD's cooperation and transparency with NGOs and international organizations, but engagement remains largely at the policy level and is far too dependent on personalities. We found that DoD is making some progress in addressing these challenges, but additional concrete steps are overdue.

Third, as with many DoD processes, civilian-harm assessment, investigation, and response should be considered part of a cycle that allows for operational and institutional learning and improvement. DoD's military services play a particularly important role in organizing, training, and equipping the force for this mission. Effective assessments and investigations of civilian harm should not only document adherence to law of war requirements but also provide a mechanism for learning that reduces civilian-harm incidents and improves mission-effectiveness across the joint force in the future. Effective assessments and investigations can also improve the extent to which forces on the ground understand the civilian environment, as well as local populations' disposition to U.S. and partner forces engaged in the area. Yet, as representatives from one command noted, lessons learned from strikes that caused civilian casualties are still not shared across all of the relevant DoD organizations in a way that is meaningfully mitigating future civilian casualties. Relatedly, they noted that their organization is not equipped to aggregate and disseminate civilian harm–related lessons learned.[7] DoD's ability to learn from its assessments, investigations, and responses to civilian-harm incidents directly affects both mitigation of future harm and mission-effectiveness.

Findings and Recommendations

In this section, we present our findings and recommendations for assessments of civilian harm, investigations of civilian harm, responses to civilian harm, and DoD resourcing and structure to address civilian harm.

Assessments of Civilian Harm

Assessing the extent and nature of civilian harm in the aftermath of military operations is critical to help the U.S. military reduce civilian harm in future operations. High-level guidance instructs U.S. government agencies to conduct assessments that "assist in the reduction of civilian casualties by identifying risks to civilians and evaluating

---

7   DoD officials, interview with the authors, May 2020.

efforts to reduce risks to civilians."[8] However, DoD's analytic and implementation processes to support such learning have not been realized.

In conducting assessments of civilian casualties and other civilian harm, the military must deal with the inherent uncertainty of determining operational outcomes in the fog of war, as well as with military and intelligence capabilities that have stark limitations in certain contexts. Air campaigns have inherent problems detecting civilian harm, given the challenges in obtaining ground truth about strikes on structures in particular. The high operational tempo and firepower used in high-intensity conflict and the limitations of U.S. control in partnered operations present their own unique dilemmas for assessments. We also found that U.S. military officials did not sufficiently engage external sources for information before concluding that reports of civilian casualties were not credible. Although DoD cannot be expected to have a perfect operational picture, it must improve its ability to draw on the best available information from both internal and external sources in order to conduct high-quality assessments.

DoD's CIVCAS cells and the CCAR process have helped ensure that each report of a civilian casualty is assessed by the U.S. military. This is indeed an improvement in the accountability and transparency of U.S. military operations, but the individual tracking of civilian-harm incidents does not necessarily mean that the U.S. military is learning lessons from those incidents.

We recommend several measures that would improve civilian-harm assessments across the spectrum of conflict. Table S.1 presents our findings in this area and the related recommendations for DoD.

Investigations of Civilian Harm

Administrative investigations have long been the most comprehensive tool for the military to document and fully understand civilian casualty incidents. However, these investigations have shortcomings that inhibit operational learning within the force.

For example, we found that the level of detail provided in investigations varied widely, creating challenges to understanding important contextual factors and analyzing root causes of civilian harm. Similar problems were noted in a 2010 study on civilian casualties and again in the 2018 Joint Staff review.[9] We also found that, unless a commander makes a concerted effort to do otherwise, investigations are typically treated as independent events, with little relationship to or learning from past investi-

---

[8]   Executive Order 13732, "United States Policy on Pre- and Post-Strike Measures to Address Civilian Casualties in U.S. Operations Involving the Use of Force," White House, July 1, 2016.

[9]   According to a joint study on civilian casualties, "there is a wide variance of facts included in legal investigation reports and in many cases these reports left out critical information necessary for operational learning" (Sarah Sewall and Larry Lewis, *Reducing and Mitigating Civilian Casualties: Afghanistan and Beyond—Joint Civilian Casualty Study*, Washington, D.C.: Joint Center for Operational Analysis and U.S. Joint Forces Command, 2010, Not available to the general public). See also Joint Staff, 2018.

Table S.1
Findings and Recommendations for Assessments of Civilian Harm

Finding	Recommendation for DoD
Air campaigns have an inherent civilian-harm detection problem.	Expand the kinds of information available for assessments to make them more robust.
Technological tools for verifying civilian harm provide an incomplete picture.	
The military's data and records that support assessments of civilian harm can be incomplete.	Develop and deploy a tool or data environment to improve collection of, access to, and storage of operational data related to civilian harm.
Military forces do not always have the ability to reconstruct the circumstances of an operation to effectively record and replay operational effects, including civilian harm.	
Intelligence efforts focus on the enemy, limiting the resources available to understand the broader civilian picture.	Incorporate civilian harm into pre-operation intelligence estimates and post-operation assessments of the cumulative effect of targeting decisions.
Incorporating the human terrain into running estimates of the operational picture during operations will assist civilian-harm assessments.	
The military's standard for finding a civilian casualty report to be credible is higher than advertised.	Use a range of estimates of civilian casualties to improve the accuracy of assessments.
The military does not always understand the civilian casualty outcomes of its partners' military operations.	Establish guidance on the responsibilities of U.S. military forces in monitoring partners' conduct and offer assistance to partners in building their own assessment capabilities if needed.
Combatant commands planning for high-intensity conflict against near-peer adversaries are unprepared to address civilian-harm issues.	Expand guidance on civilian-harm assessments across the full spectrum of armed conflict.

gations. Investigations traditionally carry a stigma of wrongdoing, and the distribution of their findings is limited. According to our interviews, even the individuals involved in an incident often never saw the results of the investigation, so they could not learn lessons from what happened. Moreover, the long timelines associated with investigations have resulted in difficulty coordinating with NGOs and have created the appearance that DoD lacks transparency, especially in cases of high-visibility reports of civilian casualties.

To offset the shortcomings of administrative investigations, we recommend implementing a standardized civilian-harm operational reporting process. Such a process could avoid the resource-intensive commitment of commander-directed investigations while also documenting and retaining critical information that can then be integrated into an effective learning process. Table S.2 presents our findings in this area and the related recommendation.

Table S.2
Findings and Recommendations for Investigations of Civilian Harm

Finding	Recommendation
The level of detail and the types of information in civilian-harm investigations vary.	Implement a standardized civilian-harm operational reporting process intended to support learning.
Investigations are treated as separate, unrelated events.	
Results of investigations are not widely disseminated.	
Investigations can carry the stigma of a disciplinary process.	
Investigations are often subject to long delays.	
Investigations have been deprioritized with the advent of the CCAR process.	
Neither investigations nor CCARs enable learning within the force.	

Responses to Civilian Harm

The U.S. military has historically found value in responding to civilian harm when it occurs. DoD's response to civilian harm can take many forms, including public acknowledgment and expressions of sympathy, livelihood assistance, restoration of damaged public infrastructure, or paying *ex gratia* to the affected community and individuals. Over the past two decades, there have been various authorities underlying DoD's ability to make *ex gratia* payments, which has led to ad hoc practices across theaters, counterproductive results, and a lack of transparency.

DoD's interim regulation on *ex gratia* payments is a step in the right direction to provide some level of standardization for responses to civilian casualties. DoD's new guidance improves consistency and transparency—for example, through maximum limits on individual payments and clearer procedures requiring commanders to document the circumstances related to a civilian casualty incident. Further improvements are needed, however, around the types of details that are released about condolence payments and the full range of response options available to commanders in the wake of civilian casualty incidents. Moreover, a response policy explicitly framed around maintaining the support of local populations where U.S. forces are operating and limited to providing condolences to those deemed friendly to the United States may not be optimized to effectively address the range of potential future conflicts.

In June 2020, DoD released an interim policy on *ex gratia* payments.[10] In Table S.3, we list our findings about DoD responses to civilian-harm incidents, including this new policy, and recommendations for further improvement.

---

[10] U.S. Under Secretary of Defense for Policy, "Interim Regulations for Condolence or Sympathy Payments to Friendly Civilians for Injury or Loss That Is Incident to Military Operations," memorandum for secretaries of the military departments, Chairman of the Joint Chiefs of Staff, and commanders of the combatant commands, June 22, 2020.

Table S.3
Findings and Recommendations for Responses to Civilian Harm

Finding	Recommendation
DoD's responses to civilian harm have historically been inconsistent and confusing.	
DoD's June 2020 interim regulation provides a new level of standardization around *ex gratia* payments.	
There are strict limits on why, where, and to whom *ex gratia* payments can be provided.	In DoD guidance, avoid placing overly restrictive limits on why, where, and to whom the U.S. military distributes condolence payments.
DoD's interim regulations lack sufficient transparency around the determination and disbursement of *ex gratia* payments.	In DoD's final policy on *ex gratia* payments, include additional transparency around how payment amounts are determined and how the payments are disbursed.
DoD's interim regulations are just part of what should be a more comprehensive response policy that addresses all civilian-harm response options.	Provide guidance and training on all options available to commanders to respond to civilian harm.

DoD Resourcing and Structure to Address Civilian Harm

DoD is not adequately organized, structured, or resourced to sufficiently mitigate and respond to civilian-harm issues. There are not enough personnel dedicated to civilian-harm issues full-time, and those who are responsible for civilian-harm matters often receive minimal training on the duties that they are expected to perform.

We found that DoD's CIVCAS cells are often staffed by junior personnel who do not receive formal training on their responsibilities, from either their commands or their military service, leaving them to learn on the job with guidance that is often insufficient. U.S. European Command and U.S. Indo-Pacific Command do not have CIVCAS cells or personnel dedicated to civilian casualty issues and are only in the early stages of thinking about how they would assess, investigate, and respond to civilian-harm issues in the event of a conflict. DoD would also benefit from additional staff with the right civilian-harm expertise in other DoD components, particularly the Office of the Secretary of Defense (OSD), the Joint Staff, and the DoD military services. Finally, DoD is missing structures and capabilities for important activities, such as analyzing and monitoring civilian-harm trends over time and archiving data. Improvements that the military has made in recent years have not necessarily translated into institutional lessons learned from those incidents.

Table S.4 presents our findings in this area and the related recommendations.

Table S.4
Findings and Recommendations for DoD Resourcing and Structure to Address Civilian Harm

Finding	Recommendation
Geographic combatant commands and other DoD components do not have sufficient dedicated, trained personnel for civilian-harm issues.	Create dedicated, permanent positions for protection of civilians in each geographic combatant command and across DoD, and establish working groups of rotating personnel for additional support.
	Create a center of excellence for civilian protection.
DoD is not organized to monitor and analyze civilian casualty trends and patterns over time.	Maintain the capability to conduct periodic reviews to monitor civilian-harm trends over time and address emerging issues.
Commands lack clear processes for assuming control of civilian casualty data and responsibilities when active operations cease.	When CIVCAS cells are established at joint task forces, define processes for reverting responsibilities and data back to the command's headquarters.

Conclusion

Many of the challenges that DoD faces in implementing these recommendations are similar to those encountered when implementing recommendations from prior studies relating to civilian harm, such as the Joint Staff's 2018 review. Continuous improvement will require DoD to view civilian-harm issues and their solutions as institutional, not just operational. Improvements in targeting, weaponeering, and other military tactics, techniques, and procedures are important but not sufficient. Institutional change in mitigating and responding to civilian harm must include improvements in such areas as data collection, learning, analysis, expertise, institutional responsibility, and evaluation of U.S. success.[11]

OSD and the Joint Staff may wish to create a roadmap, endorsed by the Secretary of Defense, for implementing the recommendations in this report, with an emphasis on institutional improvements across the joint force.

---

[11] Sarah Sewall, *Chasing Success: Air Force Efforts to Reduce Civilian Harm*, Maxwell Air Force Base, Ala.: Air Force University Press, 2016, p. 178.

Contents

Figures and Tables

Figures

Tables

CHAPTER ONE

Introduction

Study Purpose and Approach

Section 1721 of the National Defense Authorization Act (NDAA) for Fiscal Year (FY) 2020 requires that a federally funded research and development center conduct an independent assessment of U.S. Department of Defense (DoD) standards, processes, procedures, and policy relating to civilian casualties resulting from U.S. military operations. In March 2020, the Office of the Under Secretary of Defense for Policy enlisted the RAND Corporation, in collaboration with CNA, to undertake this assessment.

Section 1721 directed that this study address the following matters:

(1) Department of Defense policy relating to civilian casualties resulting from United States military operations.

(2) Standards, processes, and procedures for internal assessments and investigations of civilian casualties resulting from United States military operations.

(3) Standards, processes, and procedures for identifying, assessing, investigating, and responding to reports of civilian casualties resulting from United States military operations from the public and non-governmental entities and sources.

(4) Combatant command resourcing and organizational constructs for assessing and investigating civilian casualties resulting from United States military operations.

(5) Mechanisms for public and non-governmental entities to report civilian casualties that may have resulted from United States military operations to the Department of Defense.

(6) Standards and processes for accurately recording kinetic strikes, including raids, strikes, and other missions, and civilian casualties resulting from United States military operations.

(7) An analysis of general reasons for any disparity between third party public estimates and official United States Government estimates of civilian casualties resulting from United States or joint military operations.

(8) The standardization of dissemination and institutionalization across the Department of Defense and the combatant commands of lessons learned from United States military operations as a means of reducing the likelihood of civilian casualties from United States military operations.

(9) Any other matters the Secretary of Defense determines appropriate.[1]

DoD has a long-standing commitment to complying with the law of war and mitigating civilian harm for legal, moral, and strategic reasons and for ensuring mission-effectiveness. In 2015, DoD's Office of the General Counsel first issued the *Department of Defense Law of War Manual* to provide information on law of war concepts to personnel across the department, as well as more-specific guidance for legal advisers to operational commanders.[2] The military services also have their own manuals on the law of war.[3]

Above and beyond its law of war obligations, DoD implements policies and procedures at multiple levels to help protect civilians during armed conflict. U.S. government policy at the highest level directs departments and agencies to take measures to protect civilians in military operations. For example, Executive Order 13732, issued in 2016, directs agencies to train personnel on the protection of civilians; field weapons and intelligence, surveillance, and reconnaissance (ISR) systems that contribute to civilian protection; take feasible precautions to reduce the likelihood of civilian casualties; review incidents involving civilian casualties; acknowledge responsibility for civilian casualties and offer condolences; and engage with foreign partners to share best practices, among other measures.[4] The combatant commands also adhere to Secretary of Defense–approved and theater-specific rules of engagement, which set forth the circumstances in which force may be used, as well as the limitations on its use.

The importance of civilian protection is emphasized in U.S. military training at every level, including basic training, professional military education, and pre-deployment training. For example, U.S. Army guidance argues that, "In addition to

---

[1] Public Law 116-92, National Defense Authorization Act for Fiscal Year 2020, Section 1721, December 20, 2019.

[2] Office of the General Counsel, U.S. Department of Defense, *Department of Defense Law of War Manual*, Washington, D.C., December 2016.

[3] See, for example, Field Manual 6-27, *The Commander's Handbook on the Law of Land Warfare*, Washington, D.C.: Department of the Army and Department of the Navy, August 2019; and Air Force Instruction 51-401, *The Law of War*, Department of the Air Force, August 3, 2018.

[4] Executive Order 13732, "United States Policy on Pre- and Post-Strike Measures to Address Civilian Casualties in U.S. Operations Involving the Use of Force," White House, July 1, 2016.

humanitarian reasons and the need to comply with the law of war, excessive civilian casualties create political pressure that limits freedom of action of Army units. Civilian harm creates ill will among the population, with lasting repercussions that impair post-conflict reconstruction and reconciliation."[5]

Military commanders from the unit level to the highest headquarters in every operation speak passionately about their commitment to mitigating the risks of civilian casualties. Nevertheless, war creates competing priorities that must be balanced. How much time should the military spend assessing a report of a civilian casualty in the aftermath of a military strike in the midst of a high-intensity conflict with ongoing battles in multiple locations over many days or weeks? When do some incidents require in-depth investigations? What responsibilities does DoD have in responding to civilian casualty incidents with cash payments to victims and their families? How well trained are DoD personnel in the skills they need to assess, investigate, and respond to incidents of civilian harm? Is the vast DoD enterprise sufficiently staffed and resourced for these tasks?

DoD's efforts to understand and account for civilian harm after it has occurred—including assessments, investigations, and responses—are sometimes viewed as secondary to efforts to mitigate the risks of civilian harm in the first place. But there are important reasons to focus on improving assessments, investigations, and responses alongside mitigation. For example, **assessments** of civilian harm enable operational learning within the force and support feedback loops that can reduce civilian harm and improve mission-effectiveness. They demonstrate accountability and transparency and give the U.S. government and public a better ability to consider the costs of war. Assessments are part of the U.S. commitment to monitor its compliance with the law of war and go beyond those standards to mitigate civilian harm in future operations.

Whereas DoD performs assessments that focus primarily on determining whether civilian harm has occurred as a result of U.S. military operations, DoD may direct more-extensive **investigations** to obtain additional facts or details about a civilian-harm incident. In short, assessments tell us what happened, and investigations can tell us why. Uncovering the latter information—that is, identifying the causal factors of civilian harm—is critical in order for DoD to learn from mistakes and improve its capacity to mitigate civilian harm in the future. Investigations, if done properly, can strengthen the learning process begun by a civilian-harm assessment and can help the military institutionalize hard-earned lessons.

Responses to civilian-harm incidents can take many forms, including the provision of condolence payments to the affected community and individuals. Such responses provide assistance to those affected by the tragedy of war, advance the U.S. mission on the ground, build rapport with local communities, and reinforce the United States'

---

[5]   Army Techniques Publication 3-07.6, *Protection of Civilians*, Headquarters, Department of the Army, October 29, 2015, p. 1-3.

relationship with the host-nation government. Combatant or subordinate commands employ civilian casualty cells (CIVCAS cells) to support assessments, investigations, responses, and other issues related to civilian casualties.

Most civilian casualties caused by U.S. military operations in recent years have occurred in Afghanistan, Iraq, and Syria, and there have been fewer casualties in smaller-scale operations, such as in Somalia. In 2019, the latest year in which complete military data were available, DoD reported 22 civilians killed and 13 civilians injured in Iraq and Syria as part of Operation Inherent Resolve (OIR); 108 killed and 75 injured in Afghanistan; two killed and three injured in Somalia; and no casualties in Yemen or Libya.[6]

Many nongovernmental organizations (NGOs) work to document civilian harm in conflict zones and advocate for greater civilian protection in U.S. military operations. As we discuss in Chapter Two, estimates of civilian casualties from NGOs and other external sources have often been far higher than estimates from DoD assessments, which has been a challenge to DoD's credibility. Although some NGO personnel have expressed their respect for DoD's commitment to civilian-harm issues and the personal dedication of many U.S. service members to the issue, many other NGO representatives have expressed disappointment and surprise by a perceived lack of engagement on assessing and learning from civilian-harm incidents, particularly in the aftermath of higher-intensity battles, such as the U.S.-led coalition effort to defeat the Islamic State of Iraq and Syria (ISIS) in Raqqa, Syria.

In that battle, for example, the Combined Joint Task Force (CJTF) for OIR assessed that coalition forces were, more likely than not, responsible for 38 incidents involving 240 civilian casualties (178 killed and 62 wounded).[7] By comparison, a consortium of local Syrian and international NGOs led by Amnesty International and Airwars assessed that the number of civilian casualties ranged from 774 to 1,600, based on satellite imagery analysis, local and social media reporting, and three months of fieldwork.[8]

In this report, and using the guidelines of Section 1721 of the FY 2020 NDAA as our foundation for this study, we examine the challenges that DoD has faced in effectively assessing, investigating, and responding to civilian casualty incidents. We also analyze the challenges that DoD will likely face in more-intensive combat situations in the future. We then describe our findings and propose recommendations to help DoD overcome these challenges.

---

[6] DoD, *Annual Report on Civilian Casualties in Connection with United States Military Operations in 2019*, Washington, D.C., April 22, 2020b.

[7] See strike releases for June–October 2017 at CJTF-OIR, "Strike Releases," webpage, undated-b.

[8] Amnesty International, "War in Raqqa: Rhetoric Versus Reality," webpage, undated.

Civilian Casualty Policies and Procedures in High- Versus Low-Intensity Environments

The 2018 Joint Staff *Civilian Casualty (CIVCAS) Review* provided nine strategic recommendations for DoD to improve its ability to mitigate and account for civilian casualties resulting from U.S military operations. However, the report included an important caveat in its conclusion: "The study team acknowledges that these recommendations are primarily applicable to low to medium intensity conflicts and may also vary according to mission and specific requirements."[9] The Joint Staff study team's assumption that its civilian casualty–related recommendations had limited applicability to high-intensity conflict raises a critical question: To what extent do best practices and lessons regarding civilian harm, learned over the past 20 years of counterinsurgency (COIN) and counterterrorism operations, apply to high-intensity conflict?[10]

This question is important to answer in light of the U.S. military's current focus on high-intensity conflict. The 2018 National Defense Strategy explicitly states that "inter-state strategic competition, not terrorism, is now the primary concern in U.S. national security" and emphasizes China and Russia as immediate near-peer threats.[11] As we discuss later in this report, the two geographic combatant commands (GCCs) responsible for leading operational planning around threats emanating from China and Russia—U.S. European Command (EUCOM) and U.S. Indo-Pacific Command (INDOPACOM)—focus predominantly on preparations for high-intensity warfare. Assessing and responding to civilian harm in high-intensity conflict will clearly differ from doing so in low-intensity conflict. For example, denied or degraded environments will negatively affect the military's ability to conduct combat assessments, and expeditionary operations and communication-constrained environments will affect the flow of information related to civilians. Some of our interviewees from EUCOM and INDOPACOM expressed skepticism about the applicability of many existing civilian-harm policies, procedures, and lessons learned to their specific missions.

It is beyond the scope of this study to determine the extent to which historical best practices, lessons, and policies from low- and medium-intensity conflict apply to high-intensity conflict. That said, policymakers' and military leaders' attention to civilian harm resulting from U.S. military operations has increased over time because of a recognition that such harm is a strategic issue, as well as a moral and legal one, and an issue that influences perceptions of U.S. legitimacy and U.S. freedom of action globally. The military services also have an important role to play, including through

---

[9] Joint Staff, *Civilian Casualty (CIVCAS) Review*, Washington, D.C., April 17, 2018, p. 4.

[10] *High-intensity conflict* typically refers to war between two or more nations and their respective allies, if any, in which belligerents employ modern technology and all available resources in the domains of intelligence; mobility; firepower; command, control, and communications; and service support.

[11] DoD, *Summary of the 2018 National Defense Strategy of the United States of America: Sharpening the American Military's Competitive Edge*, Washington, D.C., 2018a, p. 1.

their professional military education programs, to prepare U.S. forces to tackle the particularly difficult challenges associated with civilian protection in high-intensity conflict. The Army's School of Advanced Military Studies and the Air Force's School of Advanced Air and Space Studies, for example, prepare strategists, planners, and military analysts to address problems with both strategic and operational aspects, which makes these schools quite relevant. The Joint Staff's Joint Advanced Warfighting School plays a similar role at the joint force level.

We thus believe that attention to civilian harm is both necessary and possible in the context of high-intensity conflict. Many of the findings and associated recommendations that we highlight in this report are applicable to high-intensity conflict, even if they will require different implementation mechanisms to account for variations in time and scale across different types of conflict. For example, a common concern is that it will be difficult, if not impossible, to investigate or assess every single potential incident of civilian harm during high-intensity conflict, making exact counts of civilians harmed largely unfeasible. We note, however, that DoD processes for accounting for the magnitude of civilian harm (e.g., civilian-harm tracking) are simply estimates based on the best information available. It is therefore not difficult to envision how DoD could still conduct civilian casualty assessments and produce estimates of civilian harm in the context of large-scale operations, even if the mechanisms and data sources are different.

Finally, despite the fact that U.S. defense strategy orients policymaker attention and resources toward Russia and China, it would be short-sighted for the military to stop planning for potential conflicts in the Middle East and Africa, where civilian casualties have most frequently occurred in this century. Indeed, many aspects of great-power competition may play out in partnership with foreign military forces in those regions rather than in head-to-head battles around Russia's or China's borders. And although many U.S. military actions since the terrorist attacks of September 11, 2001, have been in the form of deliberately planned, intensely monitored counterterrorism strikes, there have also been recent hard-earned lessons on urban battlefields—such as in Mosul, Iraq, and Raqqa, Syria—involving dynamic, fast-paced environments with artillery strikes and air strikes to defend partners under fire. Simply put, the military must institutionalize civilian harm–related lessons from past conflicts to be prepared for the new challenges of the next conflict, wherever that conflict may occur.

Study Methodology

To meet the requirements stipulated by Congress in the FY 2020 NDAA, we organized our research around four key questions:

1. How does DoD assess reported incidents of civilian harm?

2. When and how does DoD conduct more-thorough investigations, and how does this help DoD learn civilian harm–related lessons?
3. What does DoD do to respond to reports of civilian harm that it has determined to be credible?
4. How are the relevant components of DoD resourced and organized to assess, investigate, and learn from civilian harm?

In this report, we use the term *civilian harm* to include damage, injury, or death that adversely affects civilian populations, structures, or infrastructure as a consequence of military operations. We generally use *civilian casualties* in cases in which DoD is using that term, which focuses more narrowly on deaths and injuries of civilians. We also discuss the broader concept of *civilian protection*, which the U.S. Army defines as "efforts that reduce civilian risks from physical violence, secure their rights to access essential services and resources, and contribute to a secure, stable, and just environment for civilians over the long-term."[12] This last concept is important because it emphasizes the inter-connectedness among such issues as civilian casualties, civilian harm, human rights, mass-atrocity response, conflict-related sexual violence, and human security. Although we generally scope our analysis more narrowly on the problems of civilian harm, many of the solutions to these problems should be considered in the broader context of civilian protection.

To answer our four research questions, we collected and analyzed a wide variety of U.S. government documents, government and nongovernmental reports, news articles, battle histories, and operational after-action reports. We interviewed more than 80 DoD and State Department officials, military planners and operators, and NGO personnel. We also collected more than 3,000 CIVCAS credibility assessment reports (CCARs), initial assessments, civilian casualty allegation closure reports, documentation from commander-directed investigations, and military strike data for deeper analysis.[13] Analyzing a random sample of these documents enabled us to better understand the content and quality of various types of DoD reports, observe variation across time and geographical region, and compare the application of DoD's assessment standards across incidents. Through our interviews, we compared the perspectives of leaders, planners, and operators in different organizations, both within and outside DoD.

For most of our interviews, we focused on present-day policies and procedures. Where possible, we leveraged interviewees' experience in recent U.S. conflicts in Afghanistan, Iraq, Syria, and Somalia or in smaller operations. We asked interviewees—both within and outside DoD—to describe the challenges of civilian-harm assessments, investigations, and responses and about strengths and weaknesses across DoD for addressing those challenges. We sometimes performed a rudimentary process-mapping

---

[12] Army Techniques Publication 3-07.6, 2015, p. 1-1.

[13] Some of these materials, and thus some of the details of our analysis, are not publicly available.

exercise with them, asking them to use concrete examples to describe how a civilian casualty incident would be handled in their experience. Depending on the position the interviewee held, we often received vastly different perspectives, which we then cross-checked against other interviews and against the documents we had collected.

Where possible, we built on the research of past studies. The 2018 Joint Staff review, for example, analyzed a significant amount of documentation and data and conducted extensive interviews in a short period.[14] It addressed a narrow set of questions about civilian casualties resulting from several U.S.-led military operations from 2015 to 2017 and produced clear recommendations for DoD to implement. In our study, we used the Joint Staff review as a starting point but examined a wider variety of issues related to civilian harm so that we could develop a more diverse set of findings and recommendations, including an assessment of developments since 2018.

Organization of This Report

In the remainder of this report, we discuss how DoD's policies and procedures on civilian-harm assessments, investigations, and responses are applicable to high-intensity conflict environments—an important consideration in light of the changing international security environment. Chapter Two focuses on how DoD identifies and assesses incidents of civilian harm resulting from U.S. military operations and the challenges that military planners and operators face. Chapter Three examines how DoD investigates civilian-harm incidents, and Chapter Four focuses on how DoD responds to such incidents. Chapter Five analyzes the variation in structure and resourcing for addressing civilian harm at DoD and its components. Chapter Six presents recommendations for DoD policymakers, military leaders, and other stakeholders, and we assess the status of implementation of the 2018 Joint Staff recommendations. In an appendix available online at www.rand.org/t/RRA418-1, we discuss five GCCs' policies and procedures for assessing civilian casualties.

---

[14] Joint Staff, 2018, pp. 1–2.

CHAPTER TWO

Assessments of Civilian Harm

Accurate, high-quality assessments of civilian casualties in the aftermath of U.S. military operations have several important functions. First, assessments help reduce civilian casualties in future operations by identifying risks to civilians and evaluating efforts to lower those risks.[1] Assessments can also enable learning throughout the military by supporting feedback loops that improve mission-effectiveness and reduce civilian harm, if there are analytic and implementation processes in place to support such learning. Assessments can help affected civilians and their families answer important questions about the death or injury of a loved one in the aftermath of U.S. military operations. Moreover, a commitment to accurately tracking civilian harm that results from U.S. military operations demonstrates the U.S. government's accountability and transparency to victims, partner nations, and U.S. citizens. Finally, an accurate picture of civilian harm can give military leaders, political leaders, policymakers, and the public a better ability to understand and consider the costs of war.

Since approximately 2014, the U.S. military has adopted processes and procedures for assessments of civilian casualties that may have resulted from U.S. military operations. Prior to 2014, administrative investigations (the topic of Chapter Three) were primarily used for this purpose. The CCAR, described in greater detail later in this chapter, was developed in the context of OIR to allow the military to more quickly process—relative to investigations—reports of civilian casualties occurring in greater numbers and from a diverse array of external sources. These assessment procedures are now used by operational task forces in the following areas of operations: OIR in Iraq and Syria; Resolute Support (RS) in Afghanistan; operations in U.S. Central Command (CENTCOM) outside of RS and OIR, including in Yemen; and operations in U.S. Africa Command (AFRICOM). CCARs do not replace administrative investigations of civilian harm. Rather, CCARs are meant to supplement administrative investigations by providing a new tool that allows the military to more quickly assess civilian casualties at scale in environments with a higher operational tempo. The CCAR

---

[1] Executive Order 13732, 2016.

process, unlike an administrative investigation, can be automatically triggered without the discretion and direction of a commander.

In this chapter, we first describe the general processes for assessments and how these processes differ from third-party efforts to assess and monitor harm. Next, we illustrate several challenges in the assessment process based on our research. Then, we present our findings on civilian casualty assessments and argue that DoD procedures for these assessments are not sufficiently robust or consistent.

DoD Processes and Procedures for Assessing Civilian Harm During U.S. Military Operations

At the most fundamental level, the law of war requires U.S. military personnel to report possible, suspected, or alleged violations of the law. A civilian casualty does not necessarily imply that the law of war has been violated; in fact, the law of war anticipates the possibility of civilian harm and serves to limit such losses to what is proportional and ensure discrimination between targets and protected individuals and objects.[2] DoD's procedures to identify and assess civilian harm resulting from its military operations are above and beyond the requirements of the law of war.

There are two principal ways for the U.S. military to identify that it has caused civilian harm. The first way is through internal reporting from U.S. military personnel— for example, when a pilot or imagery analyst believes that he or she may have seen a civilian in the rubble following a strike. Commanders may issue command-specific guidance requiring U.S. forces to report a variety of incidents, including a civilian casualty, and military personnel can self-report civilian harm up their chain of command through such mechanisms as a serious incident report or a spot report.[3] The military may also discover civilian harm in the course of conducting a combat assessment. Chairman of the Joint Chiefs of Staff Instruction (CJCSI) 3162.02, *Methodology for Combat Assessment*, requires that commanders conduct a collateral damage assessment after a strike.[4] A collateral damage assessment is the methodological process by which the military evaluates all damage outside of the target boundary, including unintentional or incidental injury or damage to civilians, noncombatants, or their property.[5]

---

[2]   See Section 1.1 of DoD Directive 2311.01E, *DoD Law of War Program*, Washington, D.C.: U.S. Department of Defense, November 15, 2010.

[3]   Anna Khalfaoui, Daniel Mahanty, Alex Moorehead, and Priyanka Motaparthy, *In Search of Answers: U.S. Military Investigations and Civilian Harm*, Washington, D.C.: Center for Civilians in Conflict and Columbia Law School Human Rights Institute, 2020, pp. 13–14.

[4]   CJCSI 3162.02, *Methodology for Combat Assessment*, Washington, D.C.: Joint Chiefs of Staff, March 8, 2019. The CJCSI was substantially updated in 2019 to require that commanders conduct a collateral damage assessment; before that revision, such an assessment was optional but not required.

[5]   CJCSI 3162.02, 2019.

During that assessment process, analysts compare the collateral damage with the pre-strike collateral damage estimation. Collateral damage, including civilian harm, can thus be reported by operations personnel or discovered by intelligence analysts during this formal process.

The second way for the military to identify that it has caused civilian harm is through reports from external parties. In these cases, a third party observes or otherwise identifies information pertaining to what may have been an incident of civilian harm resulting from U.S. military action. Reports of civilian harm may come from members of the local civilian population, social media, journalists, or locally or remotely based NGOs and international organizations, among others. According to our interviews, the military often considers the external source's proximity to the reported civilian harm; relationship with local civilian populations; and relationship with combatant forces operating in the local area, including both U.S. military and enemy forces.[6]

Once a command receives a report of a potential civilian casualty, the assessment process is triggered to review the report and determine whether the United States was responsible for the civilian casualty. Specific processes for assessing incidents have varied over time by GCC and by operation (see the online appendix for a detailed discussion of five GCCs' processes). In general, however, there are several key steps and decision points. Figure 2.1 provides a simplified process map of the military's civilian casualty assessment process, based on written procedures from CJTF-OIR, RS, and AFRICOM.[7]

When the military receives a report of potential civilian casualties, it may compile a first-impression report or conduct an initial assessment (or both), which would include the basic facts about the reported incident (who, what, when, where, and other immediately available information), and then determine whether additional inquiry into the incident is necessary. The military may determine that no additional inquiry is necessary if, for example, there was no U.S. military action in the area of the reported incident or if a partner force was responsible for the corroborating strikes. If additional information or inquiry is required, the military will move to completing a CCAR. The military may also choose to simply open a CCAR immediately following a reported incident. The CCAR documents the information related to the incident and may include enclosures supporting its conclusions, such as full-motion video (FMV) of the

---

[6]   U.S. Marine Corps operators from tactical units, interview with the authors, March 2020, April 2020.

[7]   As detailed further in the appendix, EUCOM and INDOPACOM do not have final procedures in place to assess potential civilian casualties resulting from U.S. military operations. Personnel from both commands noted that they were waiting for the finalization of DoD policy guidance to ensure that the policies do not conflict. U.S. Southern Command (SOUTHCOM), EUCOM, INDOPACOM, and U.S. Northern Command have neither dedicated civilian casualty personnel nor a standing CIVCAS cell because of the lack of active or anticipated military conflict in their areas of responsibility (AORs), although SOUTHCOM's Human Rights Office deals with issues that fall under the broad scope of protecting civilians.

Figure 2.1
Civilian Casualty Assessment Process Map

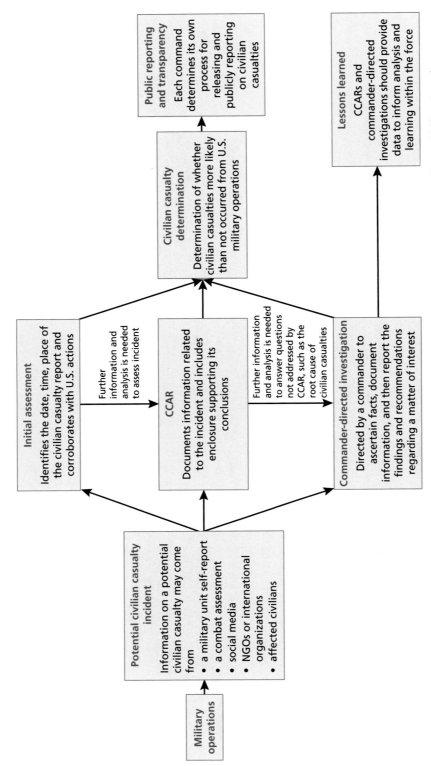

SOURCES: CJTF-OIR, *Combined Joint Task Force – Operation Inherent Resolve (CJTF-OIR) Policy for Reporting and Responding to Civilian Casualty Incidents,* Camp Arifjan, Kuwait, May 9, 2018a; and Chief, J3, "RS/USFOR-A 2019 Civilian Casualty Allegation and Mitigation Information Paper," Kabul: Headquarters Resolute Support, January 30, 2020.

incident, a combat assessment if one is available, chat logs, or strike logs. The level of detail, including the quality and number of supporting enclosures, is highly variable from CCAR to CCAR. Usually, the CIVCAS cell is responsible for coordinating the CCAR, including tasking the unit that carried out the associated strike to provide relevant information. During the CCAR process, the military will determine whether the report of civilian casualties is deemed "credible," which, according to DoD policies, means that it is "more likely than not" that civilians were injured or killed as a result of U.S. or coalition military action.[8] After the CCAR determination, a commander or other official may direct a more extensive investigation to find additional facts about the incident and to make relevant recommendations. An investigation can also be directed independently of a CCAR, in which case the command typically defers to the investigation rather than separately conducting a civilian casualty assessment.

Finally, after the military has made a determination about a reported civilian casualty, each command chooses how it will publicly report or share information about its determination. On an annual basis and as required by Section 1057 of the FY 2018 NDAA, DoD publishes a report with all credible reports of civilian casualties resulting from U.S. military operations.[9] In addition to this annual report, some commands provide additional public information on civilian casualties. Since 2016, CJTF-OIR has published a monthly civilian casualty report that highlights the status of reports from all sources, including whether the reported incidents are determined to be credible or non-credible. In March 2020, AFRICOM began releasing a similar report on a quarterly basis.[10] The RS team does not publicly release civilian casualty reports on a monthly basis or quarterly basis, opting to instead release information on a case-by-case basis. The team also releases public information on civilian casualties as part of the semi-annual report to Congress on efforts to enhance stability and security in Afghanistan, as required by Section 1225 of the FY 2015 NDAA.[11]

Third-Party Versus U.S. Military Assessments of Civilian Harm

Third-party organizations and the military have different sources and methods for identifying and assessing civilian harm resulting from U.S. military operations. These differing methodologies at times lead to dramatically different assessments of civilian

---

[8] DoD, *Department of Defense Report on Civilian Casualties in Connection with United States Military Operations in 2017*, Washington, D.C., May 22, 2018b; DoD, *Department of Defense Report on Civilian Casualties in Connection with United States Military Operations in 2018*, Washington, D.C., April 29, 2019; and DoD, 2020b.

[9] DoD, 2018b; DoD, 2019; DoD, 2020b.

[10] See, for example, U.S. Africa Command Public Affairs, "AFRICOM Civilian Casualty Status Report Initiative," press release, March 31, 2020.

[11] RS officials, interview with the authors, May 2020.

harm. Figure 2.2 illustrates such discrepancies in the estimated number of civilian deaths during U.S. military operations in Syria and Afghanistan in 2019, the latest year for which complete data were available at the time of writing.

These differing methodologies and estimates create friction during the civilian-harm assessment process, which we discuss in more detail in the next section. The U.S. military relies primarily on operational data (e.g., records of whether it conducted an operation in a given location on a given day), intelligence reporting, overhead imagery, and information from ground forces (where available), as well as some information provided by third parties. Third-party groups—which do not have access to DoD's operational data except when the military releases that information—conduct open-source conflict monitoring by leveraging local news, social media sites, and footage of incidents posted to YouTube or other outlets. NGOs (such as Human Rights Watch and Amnesty International) and international organizations (such as the United Nations Assistance Mission in Afghanistan) frequently conduct in-person interviews with victims, witnesses, medical personnel, local authorities, or community leaders to try to verify reports of civilian harm.[12] Airwars, an NGO based in the United King-

Figure 2.2
Third-Party Versus U.S. Military Estimates of the Number of Civilian Deaths in U.S. Military Operations in 2019

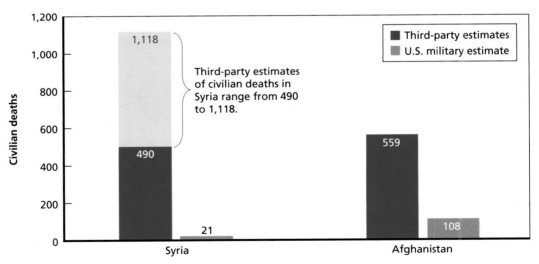

SOURCES: DoD, 2020b; Airwars, "U.S.-Led Coalition in Iraq & Syria," webpage, undated (which lists "confirmed" and "fair" incidents); and United Nations Assistance Mission in Afghanistan, *Afghanistan: Protection of Civilians in Armed Conflict 2019*, Kabul, February 2020a.

---

[12] For more information on the methodologies of the three example organizations, see Amnesty International, *"I Won't Forget This Carnage": Civilians Trapped in the Battle for Raqqa – Syria*, London, 2017, p. 8; Ole Solvang and Nadim Houry, *All Feasible Precautions? Civilian Casualties in Anti-ISIS Coalition Airstrikes in Syria*, New

dom, aggregates local media and social media reports of civilian harm and sometimes works with U.S. operational commands to provide information on specific civilian-harm incidents.

Key Findings: Assessments of Civilian Harm

The military's assessments of civilian harm are important but have limitations, which we detail in this section. Although some limitations arise from complex operational environments and the inherent uncertainty of determining outcomes in the fog of war and with limited information, others are a result of suboptimal policies and systems. The key takeaway from these findings is that DoD needs to better leverage both internal and external data to inform identification and assessment of civilian harm.

Air Campaigns Have an Inherent Civilian-Harm Detection Problem

A fundamental challenge that negatively affects the military's ability to understand and assess civilian harm that it may have caused is the United States' move toward military campaigns characterized by the use of airpower and partnered operations (such as OIR or operations in Somalia) and away from large-scale ground operations (as seen in Operation Enduring Freedom in Afghanistan or Operation Iraqi Freedom in Iraq). In military campaigns and operations that rely primarily on airpower and partnered operations, forces are less able to detect incidents of civilian harm than they are during operations with a larger ground presence. As noted in our companion report on understanding civilian harm in Raqqa, Syria,

> For example, one study identified that, during U.S. military operations in Afghanistan in 2010, air-video battle damage assessments missed civilian casualties that were later discovered during ground-led investigations in 19 of 21 cases—more than 90 percent of the time. Large-scale ground operations . . . , by contrast, have inherent advantages when it comes to detecting when civilian casualties have occurred. In [both Iraq and Afghanistan], for example, ground forces served as sensors to reveal and more precisely discern civilian harm.[13]

York: Human Rights Watch, September 24, 2017; and United Nations Assistance Mission in Afghanistan, *Afghanistan: Protection of Civilians in Armed Conflict—First Quarter Report: 1 January–31 March 2020*, Kabul, April 2020b, p. 8.

[13] Michael J. McNerney, Gabrielle Tarini, Nate Rosenblatt, Karen Sudkamp, Pauline Moore, Michelle Grisé, Benjamin J. Sacks, and Larry Lewis, *Understanding Civilian Harm in Raqqa and Its Implications for Future Conflicts*, Santa Monica, Calif.: RAND Corporation, RR-A753-1, forthcoming, p. 81. This is a companion report that focuses on civilian-harm issues during U.S. operations in Raqqa, Syria. For the study mentioned in this excerpt, see Christopher D. Kolenda, Rachel Reid, Chris Rogers, and Marte Retzius, *The Strategic Costs of Civilian Harm: Applying Lessons from Afghanistan to Current and Future Conflicts*, New York: Open Society Foundations, June 2016, p. 22.

Ground forces have also been used to investigate potential civilian casualties in greater detail through in-person site visits and witness interviews. For example, the military conducted an investigation and two inspections of an incident site after a coalition air strike in west Mosul killed 101 civilians sheltered in the bottom of a building.[14] However, site visits like this were the rare exception during OIR, in which the United States lacked a robust ground force to conduct and provide security for the investigations.

Technological Tools for Verifying Civilian Harm Provide an Incomplete Picture

In cases in which a U.S. strike matches the location and time of a civilian-harm report, the military seeks to verify whether confirmed strikes did indeed cause civilian casualties. As part of this process, the military reviews operational data (discussed in the next section) and data from FMV and ISR assets. Advances in technology have meant that the U.S. military often has a wealth of quality information, including hours of video footage from strikes, at its disposal to verify civilian casualties.

Nevertheless, these technological tools may not always be available. For example, ISR assets were in extremely high demand during OIR, leading to an overtasking of these assets and intense competition over their allocation.[15] Assets were spread thin over many missions, including target development and operational design, green-force tracking (i.e., identifying the movement of friendly forces), positive identification, close air support, and combat assessment.

Even if FMV or ISR assets are available to help assess civilian harm post-strike, there are limitations to the kind of information that the technology can collect. For example, FMV cannot record damage that occurs below an opaque surface, such as a collapsed roof; human remains buried in the rubble of a building's basement struck by an air strike would likely remain undetected. Civilian casualty data from OIR underscore these limitations of military information in some cases. The 2018 Joint Staff review examined 191 incidents of civilian casualties classified by the military as credible during OIR and noted that U.S. military sources were used to identify all but 23 of the 191 incidents.[16] The Joint Staff review also stated that reports from external sources constituted 58 percent of the total number of civilian casualties identified from 2015 to 2017.[17] This seeming discrepancy is explained by the fact that military sources tend

---

[14] Joseph Martin, Matthew Isler, and Jeff Davis, "Department of Defense News Briefing on the Findings of an Investigation into a March 17 Coalition Air Strike in West Mosul," transcript, U.S. Department of Defense, May 25, 2017.

[15] For example, CJTF-OIR Commander Sean MacFarland noted, "I had to divert resources from that fight in order to go after these targets—primarily intelligence, surveillance and reconnaissance assets. And of course, . . . any time you try to move a UAV [unmanned aerial vehicle] line someplace, there's wailing and gnashing of teeth" (Foundation for Defense of Democracies and the Brookings Institution, "Economic Defeat of the Islamic State: Behind the Scenes of Operation Tidal Wave II," panel, May 10, 2019).

[16] Joint Staff, 2018, p. 11.

[17] Joint Staff, 2018, p. 11.

to be proficient at detecting small civilian casualty incidents that involve individuals in open space or in vehicles and less proficient at identifying civilian casualty incidents caused by air strikes on structures (particularly in urban environments), which tend to cause many more casualties.

The Military's Data and Records That Support Assessments of Civilian Harm Can Be Incomplete

Another obstacle that the military faces in using the best-available information for assessments is the fact that its own internal data and records are sometimes incomplete. In its assessments, the military uses operational records, including flight logs, strike logs, targeting data, Advanced Field Artillery Tactical Data System reports (the Army's fire control reports), and other records. These are critical to conducting accurate assessments of civilian harm. However, DoD's systems and practices for managing these data and records are often insufficient to meet current requirements for civilian-harm assessments.[18]

As noted earlier, CIVCAS cells take reports of civilian casualties and compare them with the military's own records to corroborate strikes or actions. However, these records could be incomplete or inaccurate. As one U.S. operator stated, "I know from experience that data is missing, but I can't tell you how much."[19] According to military personnel interviewed for this study, the source of error in the military's records is severalfold. As outlined in our companion report,

> First, records of strikes are not automatically recorded in every case; sometimes, they are manually reported from the command executing the strike and typed by hand into a strike log, where they are subject to human error. Second, during the CCAR process, there are challenges to finding the best supporting information, including a lack of clarity surrounding which component to task for the information. For example, CJTF-OIR procedures direct the CIVCAS cell to send the request for information to whomever authorized the strike, but according to one U.S. operator, the air unit conducting or supporting the strike often has better data. In another example, the official combat assessment for strikes in the CJTF-OIR area of operations was located on a classified network that some individuals in the CIVCAS cell could not access. Finally, the military does not always archive and preserve the data it needs for civilian casualty assessments. For example, during OIR, the analysis tool that stored full-motion video from strikes was replaced with a new system, and one U.S. official had to get on a plane to another

---

[18] This point was also made in a 2010 review of civilian harm: The "requisite data [for operational learning] does not exist in an exploitable form" (Sarah Sewall and Larry Lewis, *Reducing and Mitigating Civilian Casualties: Afghanistan and Beyond—Joint Civilian Casualty Study*, Washington, D.C.: Joint Center for Operational Analysis and U.S. Joint Forces Command, 2010, Not available to the general public, p. 3). The fact that our analysis led to the same conclusion shows that this lesson from a decade ago has not yet been learned.

[19] Operational command staff, interview with the authors, June 2020.

country to retrieve a hard copy of the database. Archiving and preserving such a system is critical to having accurate assessments of civilian harm.

Difficulties accessing information were heightened when analyzing strikes that were not planned, deliberate strikes. Pre-planned strikes benefited from a wealth of information, including an intelligence package, planned weaponeering, and CDE [collateral damage estimation], all of which helped the military assess events post-strike. Air strikes taken in self-defense or collective self-defense of partner forces, however, may not have benefited from the same wealth of information. For example, the CJTF-OIR CIVCAS cell often had the most difficulty finding full-motion video and battle damage assessments for self-defense strikes.[20]

Finally, the frequent rotation of military units also made it difficult to gather quality information on old reports. Given the turnover among deployed personnel and those assigned to combatant commands, DoD's ability to reassess reported incidents when new information arises grows increasingly limited as time passes and staff with institutional knowledge and experience rotate out of an area of operations. This is important because information related to civilian casualties is often reported well after an incident occurs.

Without reliable operational data that are easily accessible to commanders, the military will be limited in its ability to understand the root causes of civilian casualties, characterize patterns of harm, and identify specific measures to mitigate civilian harm while preserving mission-effectiveness and force protection.

Military Forces Do Not Always Have the Ability to Reconstruct the Circumstances of an Operation to Effectively Record and Replay Operational Effects, Including Civilian Harm

Another limitation of the military's internal data stems from the fog of war and the fact that military forces do not always have the ability to reconstruct a mission so that its effects (e.g., a civilian-harm incident) can be analyzed for assessments or lessons learned. In general, each combatant command, component, and joint task force (JTF) uses a different system to record and store data relating to civilian harm. This is an operational and informational reality with which U.S. military personnel conducting civilian-harm assessments must contend. During OIR, for example, each echelon of the CJTF-OIR command had access to different common operational pictures because of system resolution and mission execution requirements.[21] However, this variety of

---

[20] McNerney et al., forthcoming, pp. 83–84. Many of the details from this excerpt were obtained from author interviews with operational command staff in June 2020.

[21] Per Joint Publication 3-0, a *common operational picture* is a "single identical display of relevant information shared by more than one command that facilitates collaborative planning and assists all echelons to achieve situational awareness" (Joint Publication 3-0, *Joint Operations*, Washington, D.C.: Joint Chiefs of Staff, October 22, 2018, p. GL-8). We note that, in practice, military forces tend to have operational pictures that are neither identical nor shared, a fact that has been seen to contribute to civilian casualties and friendly fire.

systems, and their design focus on supporting real-time decisions versus after-the-fact reconstruction of what happened, complicates the assessment process for determining whether civilian harm occurred and complicates the military's ability to piece together information on U.S. strikes after a civilian-harm event.

One coalition official described the difficulties inherent in reconstructing a situation after a coalition strike in Iraq that resulted in reports of civilian casualties. At the lowest echelon, special operations advisers relied on Android Tactical Assault Kit reports to monitor partner force positions and coordinate strike requests from Iraqi forces. Iraqi forces, in turn, were tracked automatically with Global Positioning System receivers and used the kit to pass coordinates, manually enter strike requests, and advise on the position of the closest friendly forces. At the strike cell echelon, coalition forces aggregated multiple subordinate echelon reports and requests onto a common operational picture that used the three-dimensional computer program Google Earth, which can incorporate new data into its satellite imagery–based geospatial platform. This program allowed coalition forces to create a complicated overlay of data that included markers for observed civilian groups, entities on a no-strike list, and intelligence reports. Finally, at the land component and CJTF-OIR headquarters levels, the coalition operated on an altogether different system.[22]

After a particularly intensive series of coalition and Iraqi strikes, there was an intricate process involved to determine whether a coalition bomb had in fact hit the structure in question and caused civilian casualties—a process that was challenging but very important to the overall mission. As the DoD official explained,

> It took a team of ten whose only job was to put together the coalition's strikes over a three-day period in a sequence that would play out like a movie. We had to rebuild the whole day—where did the ground force start? Where did all the strikes occur? We had to build a common operating picture that provided this level of information because we didn't have it. Because daily operations were so complicated, dense, and simultaneously executed at many echelons, a comprehensive picture of what happened didn't exist, even for those who participated and led advisory and strike operations. We struggled with accurate operational reconstruction and display throughout.[23]

Civilian-harm assessments seek to consolidate the best information possible, sometimes across forces, theaters, and commands. This example illustrates the significant effort that military leaders will make when they recognize the importance of assessments for mission-effectiveness and learning. Our research uncovered other examples, although none quite as in-depth as this, of military leaders successfully working to reconstruct events as part of a civilian-harm assessment. In conducting

---

[22] DoD official, interview with the authors, June 2020.

[23] DoD official, interview with the authors, June 2020.

these assessments, military personnel were at times challenged by various combinations of operational constraints, a real or perceived lack of resources, leadership inattention, and inconsistent leveraging of information sources inside and outside DoD.

Intelligence Efforts Focus on the Enemy, Limiting the Resources Available to Understand the Broader Civilian Picture

The role of intelligence in supporting the planning and execution of military operations is to reduce uncertainty and risk for commanders so that they can make decisions with the best information available at the time. Intelligence cannot provide perfect information, particularly in dynamic operating environments. In fact, when troops are in contact, ground forces may be better equipped to identify and understand a particular environment than an intelligence analyst located in a headquarters building would be. These all represent the changing facets related to the quality and quantity of both analytic support and the source of information to be analyzed throughout the estimation, planning, execution, and assessment phases of intelligence support to operations.

Multiple guidance documents point to the critical role of intelligence in mitigating civilian harm. Joint Publication 3-60, *Joint Targeting*, for example, highlights the responsibilities that the intelligence community has in informing the targeting cycle.[24] However, the focus remains on the threat from the enemy. Target intelligence briefs, target materials, battle damage estimates and assessments, and re-strike or future targeting recommendations are all examples of services that intelligence analysts provide to combat operations.[25] All of these products account for the need to mitigate civilian harm but give less emphasis to civilian-harm assessments. Post-operation combat assessments (including both battle damage assessments and collateral damage assessments) conducted by intelligence officials generally seek to assess whether the military objective was achieved or the weaponeering choice was effective and do not account for or inquire about the impact of military operations on civilians. Once a mission is deemed complete, the focus of military forces and intelligence assets turns to the next military objective rather than seeking to fully understand whether an operation resulted in civilian harm (unless a report of civilian harm is made).[26] Although CJCSI 3162.02, *Methodology for Combat Assessment*, has formalized collateral damage assessment processes, these processes can inform civilian casualty assessments effectively only if civilians are an intelligence priority on the battlefield.

---

[24] Joint Publication 3-60, *Joint Targeting*, Washington, D.C.: Joint Chiefs of Staff, September 28, 2018, Not available to the general public, p. III-9. See also CJCSI 3160.01C, *No-Strike and Collateral Damage Estimation Methodology*, Washington, D.C.: Joint Chiefs of Staff, 2018, Not available to the general public, pp. C-1, C-2, C-13, B-4.

[25] Joint Publication 3-60, 2018, p. III-10.

[26] Joint Publication 2-01, *Joint and National Intelligence Support to Military Operations*, Washington, D.C.: Joint Chiefs of Staff, July 5, 2017, p. I-1; former defense intelligence officer, interview with the authors, May 2020; and military intelligence officer, interview with the authors, June 2020.

Incorporating the Human Terrain into Running Estimates of the Operational Picture During Operations Will Assist Civilian-Harm Assessments

During operations, intelligence plays an important role in informing the commander of developments in the battlespace related to both the enemy and the human terrain.[27] These elements are incorporated into running estimates of the operational picture, which provide a commander with "a continuous assessment of the current situation" as it relates to achieving the operation's objectives, which allows the commander to determine the best course of action.[28] However, intelligence analysis and collection efforts, guided by the commander's critical information requirements and priority intelligence requirements, often prioritize understanding the enemy over understanding the civilian population. At the operational and tactical levels, priority intelligence requirements guide what information is collected and often through which method. Failing to prioritize the human terrain often leads to information gaps or the preference for technical sources of collection, such as ISR and FMV. Better utilizing all sources of intelligence collection, however, would support efforts not only to target enemies but also to understand the status of civilians. During the 2017 operations to liberate northeastern Syria from ISIS, commanders highlighted the need for better human and open-source intelligence to provide critical, detailed insights into the environment in the city of Raqqa; such insights could not be gained by national-level intelligence collection requirements or FMV. Highlighting his professional experience of the limitations of ISR, one senior U.S. military official noted that, during the battle for Raqqa, more human intelligence would have been essential to better understand the city's civilian landscape.[29]

DoD's joint targeting doctrine and manuals encourage practitioners to consider how civilians occupy the environment. However, the baseline intelligence assessment, often incorporated through the process for intelligence preparation of the operational environment, does not consider civilians as active and dynamic elements in an area of operations. Although this preparation step includes requirements to analyze the human terrain, the information required is relegated to statistics about ethnicity, economic class, political ideology, and social structures;[30] understanding these elements

---

[27] Although there is not a U.S. military doctrinal definition for *human terrain*, this idea most often refers to "the human population and society in the operational environment (area of operations) as defined and characterized by sociocultural, anthropologic, and ethnographic data and other non-geophysical information about that human population and society" (Jacob Kipp, Lester Grau, Karl Prinslow, and Don Smith, "The Human Terrain System: A CORDS for the 21st Century," *Military Review*, September–October 2006, p. 15; see also Joint Doctrine Note 4/13, *Culture and the Human Terrain*, London: U.K. Ministry of Defence, September 2013, p. 1-2). Information on human terrain is often unclassified and derived from open sources.

[28] Field Manual 6-0, *Commander and Staff Organization and Operations*, Washington, D.C.: Headquarters, Department of the Army, April 22, 2016, p. 8-1.

[29] Retired senior military officer, interview with the authors, July 2020.

[30] Joint Publication 2-01.3, *Joint Intelligence Preparation of the Operational Environment*, Washington, D.C.: Joint Chiefs of Staff, May 21, 2014, p. III-40.

does not completely lay the groundwork for mitigating civilian harm, particularly during operations. However, during OIR operations in Syria, intelligence staff leveraged all sources of information, including open-source information, to provide a current picture of the battlespace. In one instance, a general officer described that, during the battle for Raqqa, his staff built a common operational picture of pro–Syrian regime and pro–Russia force locations based on publicly available information, which was "extremely reliable."[31] In another instance, the tactical intelligence analysts supporting the battle for Raqqa leveraged Liveuamap (Live Universal Awareness Map), which uses proprietary software tools to scrape, consolidate, and map social media and other publicly available sources of information,[32] to provide the commander and operational units with updated information on the movements of civilians throughout the city and surrounding areas.[33] All-source analysts are trained to conduct such a merging of information in their assessments, but tradecraft and the battlespace commander must also emphasize the criticality of civilian-harm mitigation during operations and ensure that it is incorporated into running estimates of the operational picture. In addition to helping mitigate civilian harm, leveraging and fusing all sources of information will assist the assessment process when reports of civilian casualties arise.

The Military's Standard for Finding a Civilian Casualty Report to Be Credible Is Higher Than Advertised

The assessment process for determining whether potential civilian casualty incidents have occurred as a result of U.S. military action is a critical part of accounting for the true civilian toll of operations. As noted earlier, this assessment process considers both internal and external reports of potential civilian casualties and sets out to determine whether they were *credible*—that is, "more likely than not" to have occurred as a result of U.S. military action.[34] We found that, in some contexts—particularly for engagements of structures—the standard used for finding incidents to be credible tended to be higher than the stated standard of "more likely than not."

DoD officials note that the "more likely than not" standard is interpreted as a 51-percent probability that civilian casualties resulted from U.S. military operations.[35] This means that a finding of civilian casualties as credible is not absolute proof that civilian harm occurred but rather that such a finding is reasonable and consistent with the information available. This inherent uncertainty is consistent with the real-

---

[31] General officer, interview with the authors, August 2020.

[32] Liveuamap, "About," webpage, undated.

[33] Military intelligence analyst, email correspondence with the authors, October 2020.

[34] This standard is outlined in DoD's reporting on civilian casualties: "Under current practices and procedures, after reviewing the available information, a competent official determines whether the report of civilian casualties is 'credible,' meaning it is more likely than not that civilians were injured or killed" (DoD, 2020b).

[35] DoD official, interview with the authors, August 2020.

ity that information on the battlefield is subject to the fog of war and to limitations from both military capabilities and policy decisions. Such limitations are a result of what information capabilities can and cannot capture for a specific context, including how people and capabilities are deployed. These limitations are especially relevant for air strikes on structures during operations without ground forces. In such cases, as we noted in the previous section, the military is limited in its ability to detect civilian casualties remotely, which leads to a greater uncertainty in what actually happened in the affected structures.

For the purpose of assessments, these information limitations mean that military sources on strikes of compounds—such sources as video or images taken after an engagement—cannot necessarily be expected to show civilian casualties even if they have occurred. However, we found that, when military sources showed no evidence of civilian casualties, the U.S. military often used such findings as justification to conclude that reports of civilian casualties were not credible. Thus, the standard for deeming a civilian casualty report to be credible often required having positive proof indicating civilian harm in military information, a higher standard than the military's stated "more likely than not" standard. In addition, military sources were trusted more highly than they likely should have been, given their observed propensity to miss civilian casualties in strikes on structures.

A high-profile incident in Raqqa, Syria, illustrates this higher standard and dependence on military information in the credibility determination of the CCAR process. On March 20, 2017, U.S. forces engaged a school after determining that it was functioning as a "Daesh militant multifunctional center" and that there were 30 ISIS fighters using the school.[36] Reports of potential civilian harm from this strike arose soon after the attack, and the initial U.S. assessment (including the CCAR) found that the reports were not credible, with no military photo or video evidence to confirm that civilian harm occurred.[37] This incident was similar to other cases that we found in our review of assessments: Civilian casualties were alleged to have occurred, the military indeed attacked the alleged location, and available military information neither confirmed nor ruled out civilian casualties. Thus, these cases were determined to be not credible. The March 2017 Raqqa incident, however, shows the limitations of relying on only military information. Following the military's initial determination of this report as not credible, Human Rights Watch and the United Nations–mandated Commission of Inquiry on the Syrian Arab Republic conducted a series of on-the-ground interviews with the local population, including family members of victims. They found that civilians were living in the school at the time of the air strike, and only a few

---

[36] CJTF-OIR, "CJTF-OIR Monthly Civilian Casualty Report," press release, June 28, 2018b; and CENTCOM, "March 21: Military Airstrikes Continue Against ISIS Terrorists in Syria and Iraq," press release, No. 17-112, March 21, 2017.

[37] Airwars, "Civilian Casualties: Airwars Assessment," incident CS598, March 20, 2017.

survived.[38] When Human Rights Watch provided this additional information to the U.S. military, it reassessed the report and changed its determination to credible.[39] That the military is open to reassess its findings in light of newly identified information is a good thing. However, this example highlights the tendency of the U.S. military to dismiss external allegations without the "smoking gun" of military information, only to backtrack and reverse a determination of not credible that was made when the military could neither confirm nor deny that civilian casualties had occurred.

Our analysis of military assessments also revealed evidence to suggest that this higher credibility standard was applied in several cases prior to the discovery of all available military information. In these cases, the military initially made the decision to find an incident not credible. Then, additional military imagery or video of the incident was provided that showed positive evidence of civilian casualties. In each of these cases, there was an engagement on a structure, and the military had confirmed that the United States had indeed engaged the structure in question. The only uncertainty was whether civilian harm had occurred inside the structure. The discovery of additional military information confirming civilian casualties led to a reversal of these incidents from not credible to credible.[40]

These two cases demonstrate that the U.S. military is striving to deal with a hard problem: the inherent uncertainty of determining operational outcomes, given the fog of war and military capabilities that have stark limitations in certain contexts. However, the military's "more likely than not" criteria is, in practice, not sufficiently articulated in military documentation, guidance, or training to inform those who are using it for assessments. Thus, the decisionmaking criteria, as illustrated earlier, result in a systemic under-counting of civilian casualties in some cases.

The Military Does Not Always Understand the Civilian Casualty Outcomes of Its Partners' Military Operations

The United States rarely conducts military operations without the support of other countries. Although a full discussion on civilian casualty reporting in coalition and partnered operations is outside the scope of this study, it is important to briefly highlight how the U.S. military works with partners to assess possible civilian casualties that occur during operations. When operating within a coalition, the U.S. military works with its allies to track the collective contributions to civilian harm. The information is not necessarily all released to the public, but the details include a record of specific incidents of civilian harm, the nation that was responsible, whether the mili-

---

[38] Solvang and Houry, 2017; and United Nations, *Report on the Independent International Commission of Inquiry on the Syrian Arab Republic*, New York, A/HRC/37/72, February 1, 2018.

[39] CJTF-OIR, 2018b.

[40] The CCARs that we reviewed, and thus some of the details of our analysis, are not publicly available.

tary has deemed it credible that civilian harm resulted from coalition operations, and the estimated civilian harm from the incident.

The United States does not take the same approach with partner-nation forces that it assists—for example, Iraqi or Afghan security forces or local militias. This can lead to an accountability gap, in which harm caused by local forces—who might be armed, trained, or supported by the United States—cannot be identified or mitigated. U.S. engagement with forces that cause civilian harm may alienate local populations and reduce U.S. credibility in the region and globally. For example, in Mosul and other counter-ISIS operations in Iraq, the CJTF-OIR CIVCAS cell would assess possible civilian casualty incidents, and if an incident could not be matched with a coalition attack but was possibly a result of an Iraqi military action, the coalition would forward the details of the incident to the Iraqis. However, the coalition would not follow up on the incident to see what the Iraqis determined or attempt to independently track the number of incidents or the magnitude of civilian harm caused by the Iraqis. Furthermore, the United States did not work with the Iraqis to help them develop their own ability to track and assess civilian harm.

Similarly, the United States provided weapons, intelligence, and advisory support to the Saudi-led coalition in Yemen starting in 2015. When civilian harm from the Saudi-led coalition became a significant concern, the United States increased its advisory support, including on targeting best practices and the law of war. Civilian-harm tracking was not one of the advisory topics; however, from approximately October 2017 to November 2019, the advisory team from U.S. Air Forces Central included weekly reports of observed civilian casualties from Saudi-led coalition operations.[41] This information would generally not be reported above the component level unless it met certain criteria, such as a law of war violation or a large civilian casualty incident.[42]

Overall, despite the potential for civilian harm in partnered operations, the U.S. military has not considered it a responsibility to track or build capability for civilian-harm tracking with partners (although there are nascent efforts by the Defense Security Cooperation Agency to help partners develop their own capability).[43] However, there may be cases in which partner forces and their leadership are opposed to the United States tracking and reporting on incidents of partner-caused civilian harm. This does not necessarily imply bad intent; to track and evaluate incidents, the U.S. military would need to be privy to a great deal of information, often classified and sensitive. Heavy-handed efforts by U.S. forces to track civilian harm could backfire. For instance, partners could lose trust in the United States, or the U.S. military could lose the partner's support, potentially putting U.S. objectives at risk or causing worse

---

[41] Larry Lewis, *Promoting Civilian Protection During Security Assistance: Learning from Yemen*, Arlington, Va.: CNA, May 2019b; and former general officer, interview with the authors, January 2021.

[42] Former general officer, interview with the authors, January 2021.

[43] DoD official, interview with the authors, January 2021.

behavior from partner forces. Thus, in working with partners, U.S. officials might choose to forgo official tracking and reporting, although cases of law of armed conflict violations should always be reported. In all partnered operations, however, DoD should take responsibility for ensuring that partner forces are trained in civilian-harm mitigation and assessments and that they are taking these actions either independently or with U.S. assistance.

Combatant Commands Planning for High-Intensity Conflict Against Near-Peer Adversaries Are Unprepared to Address Civilian-Harm Issues

Our research shows that there is significant variation in the extent to which GCCs are prepared to address civilian-harm issues. In particular, interviews with personnel from INDOPACOM and EUCOM suggest that existing policies and procedures around civilian casualty assessments are insufficient to meet the challenges of high-intensity conflict. DoD's military services also play an important role in organizing, training, and equipping the force to conduct civilian-harm assessments. Moreover, planners and operators assigned to INDOPACOM and EUCOM have publicly expressed concern over the extent to which civilian casualty–related lessons learned from COIN and counterterrorism operations apply to contexts of great-power conflict. Differences in the pace of operations, the nature and use of munitions, the relative balance of air versus ground assets, and the strategic value of civilians all highlight the need for scalable guidance that can translate to the full spectrum of war.

During the course of our research, interviewees in INDOPACOM and EUCOM consistently referred to great-power conflict or high-intensity conflict without specifying what that would look like in their AORs. However, the unspoken assumption appeared to be that this type of conflict could involve large numbers of civilian casualties as a result of operations in the vicinity of or directly targeting large urban areas. Indeed, a 2020 RAND study suggests that any future conflict involving Russia, China, and the United States is likely to unfold in more-urbanized contexts, making it harder for militaries in general—and airpower in particular—to discriminate between military and civilian targets and conduct assessments in the wake of incidents of civilian harm.[44] It is also likely that Russia and China would heavily politicize incidents of civilian harm caused by the United States in an effort to portray it in the most negative light possible, complicating investigations and response more generally. The INDOPACOM AOR in particular lacks the presence of independent civil society organizations that could provide incident-specific or contextual details that inform assessments. Moreover, during high-intensity conflict operations, reliable, all-source intelligence is critical. However, the battles for Mosul and Raqqa illustrated that, during operations

---

[44] Raphael S. Cohen, Nathan Chandler, Shira Efron, Bryan Frederick, Eugeniu Han, Kurt Klein, Forrest E. Morgan, Ashley L. Rhoades, Howard J. Shatz, and Yuliya Shokh, *The Future of Warfare in 2030: Project Overview and Conclusions*, Santa Monica, Calif.: RAND Corporation, RR-2849/1-AF, 2020, p. 33.

in urban areas, dedicating days of ISR to develop pattern of life is a luxury that may not exist. In short, many of the challenges around assessing civilian harm identified previously in this chapter would likely be heightened in contingencies against near-peer adversaries.

As we discuss later in this report, EUCOM and INDOPACOM are taking preliminary steps toward developing guidance and policy that will better prepare them to face these and other civilian casualty–related challenges should high-intensity conflict break out in their AORs. They also conduct training and operations in areas relevant to civilian protection, such as humanitarian assistance and disaster response, which could provide a baseline from which U.S. military forces in these regions could build on existing capabilities to tailor them to respond to potential future civilian casualty incidents. Although these are steps in the right direction, INDOPACOM and EUCOM remain largely unprepared to holistically address civilian-harm issues in their respective regions.

Conclusion

The U.S. military has extensive processes for conducting assessments of civilian-harm incidents, but there is room for improvement. In conducting these assessments, the military is dealing with the inherent uncertainty of determining operational outcomes in the fog of war and with military and intelligence capabilities that have stark limitations in certain contexts. Air campaigns have inherent problems detecting civilian harm, given the challenges in obtaining ground truth about strikes on structures, in particular. The high operational tempo and firepower used in high-intensity conflict and the limitations of U.S. control in partnered operations present their own dilemmas for assessments. When military sources showed no evidence of civilian casualties—often because they did not put forth sufficient effort to engage external sources—the U.S. military often used such findings as justification to conclude that reports of civilian casualties were not credible. Although DoD cannot be expected to have a perfect operational picture, it must improve its ability to draw on the best-available information from both internal and external sources in order to conduct high-quality assessments.

CHAPTER THREE

Investigations of Civilian Harm

The CCAR process described in the previous chapter focuses primarily on determining whether civilian harm has occurred as a result of U.S. military action. Although this assessment is important, more information is needed for the military to be able to learn and improve. The military has sophisticated practices and tools to help anticipate and mitigate civilian harm, but it has few tools and institutional structures for identifying civilian harm–related lessons and learning from them.[1] Historically, DoD's primary tool for learning from civilian-harm incidents has been commander-directed investigations, referred to here as *investigations.*

Investigations can be directed by a commander or other DoD official to obtain additional facts about civilian-harm issues or incidents through an appointing order. As noted in our companion report, "Although different DoD components can have different investigation procedures (e.g., in an Air Force commander-directed investigation or an investigation subject to the Navy and Marine Corps Manual of the Judge Advocate General), Army Regulation [AR] 15-6 investigations are the most commonly used in recent joint operations."[2] An AR 15-6 investigation is used as the basis for many formal and informal investigations requiring the detailed gathering and analysis of facts and the development of recommendations.[3]

Investigations are an important learning tool for the military and can be used to help address a wide variety of topics. Over the past 15 years, investigations have been a significant part of the lessons-learned process for civilian casualties. For example, several commanders in Afghanistan and U.S. special forces commanders mandated that every potential civilian casualty incident would be the subject of an investigation because they wanted to take every opportunity to learn and improve. Because these investigations documented specific incidents in detail, they were conducted in addition to other reporting and assessment processes in place. This provided a foundation

---

[1] Joint Center for Operational Analysis, *Adaptive Learning for Afghanistan: Final Recommendations,* Suffolk, Va.: U.S. Joint Forces Command, February 10, 2011, Not available to the general public.

[2] McNerney et al., forthcoming, p. 79.

[3] Army Regulation 15-6, *Procedures for Administrative Investigations and Boards of Officers,* Washington, D.C.: Headquarters, Department of the Army, April 1, 2016, pp. 1–2.

for the military to better understand the causal factors of civilian harm and identify specific ways to change command guidance and tactics, techniques, and procedures to reduce the risk of civilian harm. Although commander-directed investigations have historically been the best way of documenting specific incidents for learning purposes compared with other methods available (e.g., CCARs), the investigation process was not always compatible with specific requirements for learning from civilian casualty incidents.

Key Findings: Investigations of Civilian Harm

Investigations—long the most comprehensive tool for the U.S. military to document instances of civilian casualties—have some significant shortcomings. Our key findings in this area include five shortcomings and two more-overarching observations.

The Level of Detail and the Types of Information in Civilian-Harm Investigations Vary

The first of these shortcomings, which was highlighted in the 2018 Joint Staff review on civilian casualties, was that "the details and information included in each [AR 15-6] report and alignment with ongoing NGO investigations vary."[4] This variance makes it more difficult to learn from individual incidents when relevant factors are not systematically included. The Joint Staff study team recommended a step that has yet to be taken by DoD: "The U.S. military should institutionalize [civilian casualty] investigation processes. This should include sharing best practices in AR 15-6 adjudication and public release, as well as closer engagement with NGOs during this process, where feasible."[5] Similar problems of varying information and detail were noted in a 2010 study on civilian casualties.[6] These observations were the basis for the inclusion of Appendix B in Army Tactics, Techniques, and Procedures 3-37.31, which gives suggested data elements for investigations of civilian casualty incidents to facilitate learning.[7] However, our inspection of later investigation reports indicates that—more than a decade later—these suggested standards have not yet been adopted.

---

[4]   Joint Staff, 2018, p. 12.

[5]   Joint Staff, 2018, p. 14.

[6]   According to the joint study, "there is a wide variance of facts included in legal investigation reports and in many cases these reports left out critical information necessary for operational learning" (Sewall and Lewis, 2010).

[7]   Army Tactics, Techniques, and Procedures 3-37.31, *Civilian Casualty Mitigation*, Washington, D.C.: Headquarters, Department of the Army, July 2012.

Investigations Are Treated as Separate, Unrelated Events

The second shortcoming of investigations is that, unless a commander makes a con-certed effort to do otherwise, investigations are typically treated as independent events, with little relationship to or learning from past investigations.[8] This is a problem because lessons are most valuable when they are collated, validated, and put in context. For example, after an inadvertent strike on a Médecins Sans Frontières/Doctors With-out Borders hospital in Afghanistan in 2015, the U.S. military developed a detailed investigation looking into the incident. However, the investigation process did not consider past incidents of civilian casualties, thus failing to recognize that many of the causal factors had been seen before, were chronic challenges for the military, and were not unique to the case of this medical facility.[9] This was a lost opportunity for learn-ing. In contrast, when the U.S. military has made efforts to gather sets of investiga-tions and analyze them, that process has often identified issues that were not noticed in individual investigation reports; in such cases, it became easier to see the forest and not just the trees.[10]

Results of Investigations Are Not Widely Disseminated

Third, investigation reports are considered sensitive and typically held within legal channels. This limits their wide dissemination to other units, and even more so to U.S. allies, complicating how useful investigations can be as tools for learning. For example, when senior leaders in Afghanistan directed a study in 2009 leveraging all of the inves-tigations on civilian casualties from the previous few years, the study team had to go to the legal staff at all of the different relevant commands. The investigation reports were not centrally available, and the study team even received warnings from lawyers about limiting the reports' dissemination. This limited distribution was even true for units involved in the incidents in question; interviewees indicated that they usually never saw the results of investigations of incidents that they were involved with so that they could learn lessons from what happened.[11]

Investigations Can Carry the Stigma of a Disciplinary Process

Fourth, investigations can carry connotations of wrongdoing, which is generally unhelpful because the vast majority of U.S.-caused civilian casualties either have been accidents or were accepted casualties within the realm of proportionality, in which civil-

---

[8] Several interviewees made this point to us, including two who personally made special efforts to leverage investigations for learning (military leaders and former operators, interview with the authors, April 2020, May 2020).

[9] U.S. Forces Afghanistan, *Investigation Report of the Airstrike on the Médecins Sans Frontières/Doctors Without Borders Trauma Center in Kunduz, Afghanistan on 3 October 2015*, April 28, 2016.

[10] Larry Lewis, "We Need an Independent Review of Drone Strikes," *War on the Rocks*, May 6, 2015.

[11] Current and former military operators, interview with the authors, April 2020, May 2020.

ians were harmed without U.S. forces violating the law or commander's guidance. Our interviews of military personnel generally revealed apprehensive attitudes about investigations. And this apprehension appeared to be warranted: Even though investigation reports have a stated purpose of learning, several reports recommended disciplinary action for personnel involved in civilian casualty incidents when those personnel were found to have violated guidance or procedures or to have shown poor judgment.[12]

Investigations Are Often Subject to Long Delays

The fifth shortcoming that we identified is that investigations tend to take a long time, conflicting with DoD's goal of responding to external reports of potential civilian casualties in a timely manner. Interviewees noted that these delays result in difficulty coordinating with NGOs and create the appearance that DoD lacks transparency, including with high-visibility reports of civilian casualties.[13] This appearance of a lack of transparency is compounded by the lack of a policy or common approach to the public release of investigations. Such release is a case-by-case decision; some redacted reports are released in their entirety (typically for high-profile cases), and others are not released at all or only the executive summary is made public.

Concern by NGO personnel and other civilian stakeholders about delays is also a symptom of another problem: a general lack of engagement with civil society. Civil society actors have access and information that DoD may lack, as well as important perspectives that may challenge conventional wisdom and reduce the risk of groupthink. Given the previously mentioned finding from the 2018 Joint Staff review that 58 percent of acknowledged civilian harm originated from civil society and other external sources, investigations would benefit from engaging with civil society to maximize the consideration of all available information.

Investigations Have Been Deprioritized with the Advent of the CCAR Process

Some of these challenges with investigations led DoD to develop the streamlined CCAR process discussed in Chapter Two. Through our research, we found that the use of CCARs has had some unanticipated consequences. For example, whereas U.S. military forces in Afghanistan generally required an investigation for each civilian casualty incident, CJTF-OIR commanders relied on CCARs to document most incidents. This approach prioritized speed and the minimization of resources but sacrificed the learning that is enabled by documentation and detail about individual incidents. Relying on the more limited detail and scope of CCARs without also conducting investigations or some other detailed documentation of what happened and why creates a gap in knowledge.[14] CCARs can be helpful when facts need to be known

---

[12] Sewall and Lewis, 2010.

[13] DoD officials, interview with the authors, May 2020.

[14] See, for example, Khalfaoui et al., 2020, p. 35.

quickly and when there are many potential incidents being reported, but CCARs should not result in avoiding investigations when that level of scrutiny is necessary. Military commanders should regard investigations as a tool in their broader tool-kit intended to help inform the art of command and to promote operational learning. Some commanders may be more deliberate about pursuing this kind of process than others are, but it should not be dependent on a given leader. By leaving the use of investigations to the discretion of the commander without sufficient guidance or direction about when and how to use them, it is too easy for busy military leaders to give investigations insufficient priority.

Neither Investigations nor CCARs Enable Learning Within the Force

Finally, both investigations and CCARs are a poor fit when it comes to enabling learning within the force. When U.S. and international forces in Afghanistan struggled with a rising civilian toll that became a strategic issue affecting the overall campaign, a set of periodic reviews between 2009 and 2012 helped identify emerging issues regarding civilian harm and address them in a timely way. These reviews used data captured in investigations and other military reports to identify root causes and patterns responsible for incidents of civilian harm, which enabled military forces to tailor adaptations to reduce risks to civilians. This data-driven approach led to reductions in both numbers and rates of civilian harm in the Afghanistan campaign.[15]

This learning approach was suggested in Section 4 of Executive Order 13732, in which the U.S. government makes a commitment to monitor civilian casualty trends over time so that it can mitigate and respond to them as needed.[16] The U.S. government has not fulfilled this policy commitment, and it is likely that this has had a tangible cost to the United States in its efforts to protect civilians.[17] DoD can do this monitoring and trend analysis independently of other federal agencies, but it has not taken this step in recent operations. For example, the 2018 Joint Staff review found that, during U.S. and coalition operations in Iraq and Syria, the civilian casualty rate increased sharply over a few years with no targeted monitoring or mitigation efforts in response to that clear undesirable trend.

---

[15] Larry Lewis, *Reducing and Mitigating Civilian Casualties: Enduring Lessons*, Washington D.C.: Joint and Coalitional Operational Analysis, April 12, 2013.

[16] Executive Order 13732, 2016.

[17] Larry Lewis, "Reflecting on the Civilian Casualty Executive Order: What Was Lost and What Can Now Be Gained," *Just Security*, March 12, 2019a.

Conclusion

U.S. military investigation processes fall short in supporting a learning approach to civilian harm. Although investigations have historically been the most comprehensive tool for the military to document and better understand civilian casualty incidents, their substantial shortcomings—including an uneven level of detail, limited distribution, associated stigma, delays, and relative deprioritization in recent years—inhibit operational learning within the force. In Chapter Six, we propose a new approach to reporting and investigations specifically for the purpose of learning.

CHAPTER FOUR

Responses to Civilian Harm

The U.S. military has historically found value in responding to civilian harm when it occurs. DoD's response to civilian harm can take many forms, such as publicly acknowledging the incident and expressing sympathy, releasing public information about the incident, communicating about U.S. decisions in military operations, providing livelihood assistance to victims, restoring damaged public infrastructure, and paying condolences to the affected community and individuals. Such responses to civilian harm caused by U.S. military operations serve several purposes. First, they can help the U.S. mission on the ground by protecting the reputation and legitimacy of the United States and its actions. Second, they can build rapport with local communities affected by U.S.-caused civilian harm, which was an important part of the United States' COIN strategy in Iraq and Afghanistan. Third, these responses can reinforce the United States' relationship with the host-nation government. Finally, they can provide assistance to those affected by the tragedy of war, consistent with U.S. values and principles.

Historically, there have been various authorities underlying DoD's ability to provide condolence payments, but the common factor among them is that these payments are made *ex gratia*—that is, they are made without DoD recognizing any legal obligation to provide the assistance. International and U.S. laws do not obligate the United States to pay compensation for civilians harmed in the midst of lawful combat operations, and any payments that the military makes are not meant as formal reparation or an admission of fault or negligence. The 1942 Foreign Claims Act created a system to adjudicate claims of civilian-harm caused by *non*-combat, negligent, or wrongful actions; however, the act includes a "combat exclusion" clause that specifically prohibits commanders from using the act to compensate victims of civilian harm resulting from U.S. military operations.[1] Despite these legal restrictions, the United States has maintained an ad hoc ability to provide condolence payments as a gesture of sympathy given to acknowledge and ease civilian suffering resulting from U.S. military operations.

---

[1] U.S. Code, Title 10, Section 2734, Property Loss; Personal Injury or Death: Incident to Noncombat Activities of the Armed Forces; Foreign Countries.

In recent conflicts, the lion's share of *ex gratia* payments have been paid to civilians in Afghanistan. According to information released by U.S. Army Central, $4.8 million was disbursed in condolence payments to Afghan nationals between 2005 and 2014.[2] Figures 4.1 and 4.2 provide some insight into the *ex gratia* payments made in Afghanistan between 2015 and 2019, but the data are limited because DoD, in accordance with congressional requirements, began to publicly report the number and value of payments only in early 2020 for payments made during 2019. In August 2020, in response to media requests, DoD also publicly released data on *ex gratia* payments made in Afghanistan from 2015 to 2019.[3]

Figure 4.1 shows the number of *ex gratia* payments disbursed in Afghanistan from 2015 to 2019, according to DoD's publicly available data. We include *condolence payments* (defined as payments to civilians who were killed, were injured, or incurred property damage as a result of U.S. actions during combat) and *battle damage payments* (defined as payments to repair damage that results from U.S., coalition, or support-

Figure 4.1
Number of *Ex Gratia* Payments Made in Afghanistan and Iraq, 2015–2019

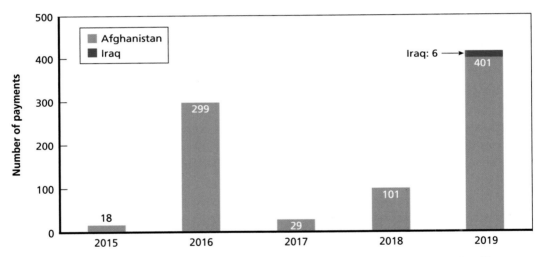

SOURCES: Data provided to RAND by OSD officials in September 2020; and Missy Ryan, "U.S. Military Made $2 Million in Civilian Casualties Payments in Afghanistan in Recent Years," *Washington Post*, August 17, 2020.
NOTE: Totals include battle damage payments and condolence payments.

---

[2] Center for Civilians in Conflict, "Ex-Gratia Payments in Afghanistan: A Case for Standing Policy for the US Military," issue brief, May 11, 2015.

[3] The data were released in response to a media request for the sake of transparency (DoD official, interview with the authors, November 2020).

ing military operations that is not compensable under the Foreign Claims Act).[4] DoD has not publicly reported any payments made in Iraq prior to 2019 or any payments in Syria, Yemen, or Somalia, but civil society organizations claim that DoD paid four *ex gratia* payments in the context of CJTF-OIR, including one payment in Syria for a strike in 2019.[5]

Figure 4.2 shows the fluctuations in average *ex gratia* payment amounts in Afghanistan over this same period. Available data from Iraq are not shown in this chart, but $24,000 in condolence payments were disbursed in Iraq in 2019, averaging $4,000 per payment.[6]

Figure 4.2
Average Value and Range of *Ex Gratia* Payments in Afghanistan, by Payment Type, 2015–2019

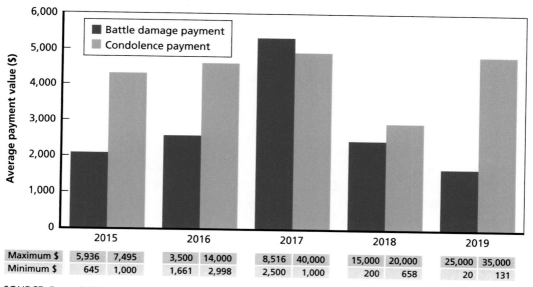

	2015		2016		2017		2018		2019	
Maximum $	5,936	7,495	3,500	14,000	8,516	40,000	15,000	20,000	25,000	35,000
Minimum $	645	1,000	1,661	2,998	2,500	1,000	200	658	20	131

SOURCE: Ryan, 2020.

[4] Sharon L. Pickup, Carole F. Coffey, Kelly Baumgartner, Krislin Bolling, Alissa Czyz, K. N. Harms, Ronald La Due Lake, Marcus L. Oliver, and Jason Pogacnik, *Military Operations: The Department of Defense's Use of Solatia and Condolence Payments in Iraq and Afghanistan*, Washington, D.C.: U.S. Government Accountability Office, May 1, 2007.

[5] NGO official, interview with the authors, November 2020; Airwars [@airwars], "Recently we learned from @DeptofDefense that 611 ex gratia payments . . . ," Twitter post, June 24, 2020; and Human Rights Watch, "Syria: U.S. Coalition Should Address Civilian Harm," July 9, 2019.

[6] Ryan, 2020.

Key Findings: Responses to Civilian Harm

DoD's Responses to Civilian Harm Have Historically Been Inconsistent and Confusing

Over the past two decades, DoD's procedures for responding to civilian-harm incidents have been inconsistent and confusing to both military commanders and civil society organizations. Until June 2020—nearly two decades after the military began providing condolence payments in Iraq and Afghanistan—there was no uniform DoD framework for providing payments to victims when the U.S. military caused civilian casualties. Prior to this, commanders generally used two mechanisms to provide *ex gratia* payments. Solatia payments were funded from a military unit's operations and maintenance accounts and were required to be paid in accordance with local customs.[7] Solatia payments were made in Iraq from June 2003 to January 2005 and have been made in Afghanistan since October 2005.[8] Other payments in contrast were primarily paid from the Commander's Emergency Response Program, a system first created in Iraq in 2004. The ability to use this program for *ex gratia* payments was subsequently extended to Syria, Somalia, Libya, and Yemen (though such payments have been either rare or non-existent in these countries).[9]

This piecemeal approach resulted in ad hoc and inconsistent practices for the disbursement of *ex gratia* payments across different theaters. Commanders have regularly taken creative license to distribute resources that are intended for a different purpose—for example, to assist in reconstruction efforts or other activities that fall into the scope of COIN or stability operations.[10] Previous research has documented significant disparities between condolence decisions and payment amounts across similar cases in the same country, making the overall process unpredictable and confusing for affected

---

[7] Pickup et al., 2007.

[8] Daniel R. Mahanty, Jenny McAvoy, and Archibald S. Henry, *The U.S. Military and Post-Harm Amends Policy and Programs: Key Considerations and NGO Recommendations*, Washington, D.C.: Center for Civilians in Conflict, March 2019, p. 7.

[9] Marla B. Keenan and Jonathan Tracy, *US Military Claims System for Civilians*, Washington, D.C.: Center for Civilians in Conflict, 2008. The authority to use the Commander's Emergency Response Program expired in Iraq in 2011 (Administrator of the Coalition Provisional Authority, "Commanders' Emergency Response Program," memorandum to the Commander of Coalition Forces, June 16, 2003). Following the rise of ISIS, Congress reauthorized the program for the use of condolence payments in 2016 for Iraq under section 2111 of the FY 2016 NDAA; for Syria under Section 2111 of the FY 2017 NDAA; and for Somalia, Libya, and Yemen under Section 1224 of the FY 2018 NDAA.

[10] As one member of the Army Judge Advocate General's Corps noted, "due to the [Foreign Claims Act's] limitations, commanders . . . have frequently engaged in legal and fiscal gymnastics to find a way to express condolence for harm caused to civilians arising out of combat activities" (Katharine M. E. Adams, "A Permanent Framework for Condolence payments in Armed Conflict: A Vital Commander's Tool," *Military Law Review*, Vol. 224, No. 2, 2016, p. 320).

civilians.[11] *Ex gratia* payments have also resulted in unintended or undesirable consequences, such as the public rejection of payments after U.S. air strikes inadvertently hit a hospital in Kunduz, Afghanistan.[12] Moreover, the extent to which U.S. forces have made condolence payments to civilian victims of U.S. military operations has fluctuated significantly across conflicts, adding to the aura of incoherence and inviting more criticism from outside parties. For example, large numbers of condolences paid to civilian victims during U.S. military operations in Afghanistan and Iraq in the 21st century created the expectation among civil society organizations that the military will typically pay *ex gratia* when it takes responsibility for harming civilians in military operations. When payments fell significantly for OIR operations, DoD was subject to criticism. According to one official we interviewed, "We've given so much *ex gratia* in Afghanistan and in Iraq that we've created the expectation that it will always be paid. In OIR, we made so few *ex gratia* payments because we didn't have many boots on the ground."[13] In short, DoD has struggled to publicly communicate a clear and consistent message about why and when *ex gratia* payments are provided to civilians who are harmed by U.S. military operations.

DoD's June 2020 Interim Regulation Provides a New Level of Standardization Around *Ex Gratia* Payments

In June 2020, the Under Secretary of Defense for Policy issued a memorandum called "Interim Regulations for Condolence or Sympathy Payments to Friendly Civilians for Injury or Loss That Is Incident to Military Operations," which provided more structure to the process for providing *ex gratia* payments to civilians harmed as a result of U.S. military operations.[14] The regulations contain procedural guidance to U.S. military commanders for issuing payments under the authority of the FY 2020 NDAA, Section 1213, titled "Authority for Certain Payments to Redress Injury and Loss" (hereafter referred to as Section 1213).[15] The regulations focus primarily on reporting and documentation guidance, standard payment levels, and the roles and responsibilities of relevant DoD components. The memorandum also notes that funds for *ex gratia* payments will be drawn from funds appropriated to OSD under the DoD-wide operations and maintenance account, marking a departure from the use of previous funding

---

[11] Center for Civilians in Conflict, 2015.

[12] Philip Reeves, "Survivors of Afghan Hospital Airstrike Dissatisfied with Compensation Plan," NPR, April 11, 2016.

[13] DoD official, interview with the authors, May 2020.

[14] U.S. Under Secretary of Defense for Policy, "Interim Regulations for Condolence or Sympathy Payments to Friendly Civilians for Injury or Loss That Is Incident to Military Operations," memorandum for secretaries of the military departments, Chairman of the Joint Chiefs of Staff, and commanders of the combatant commands, June 22, 2020.

[15] Pub. L. 116-92, 2019.

sources, such as the Commander's Emergency Response Program or military units' operations and maintenance accounts. Although the interim regulations focus exclusively on payments, as opposed to other forms of response, they do briefly note that such payments are one of several options to be considered for responding to civilian harm. Other possible response options may include "public acknowledgment that the property damage, personal injury, or death was incidentally caused by U.S. forces; medical care to the extent authorized by law; or other appropriate measures that may be consistent with mission objectives and applicable law."[16] The interim regulations state an expectation that a permanent policy will be in place by February 2022.

The interim regulations improve upon DoD's past policy and procedures in that they introduce more standardization and transparency around *ex gratia* authorities, procedures, and amounts to be disbursed to victims of civilian-harm incidents. Moreover, the regulations open the door to the development of a more inclusive and consultative condolence process by specifying that combatant commanders are responsible for conducting regional or country-specific assessments of cultural appropriateness, economic conditions, and other factors relevant to establishing local condolence programs. Finally, the regulations expand eligibility for *ex gratia* payments to civilians harmed in the course of coalition- or partner-led operations.

There Are Strict Limits on Why, Where, and to Whom *Ex Gratia* Payments Can Be Provided

DoD's interim regulations on *ex gratia* payments impose limits on why, where, and to whom payments can be disbursed. Section 1213 notes that payments may be provided only to civilians who are "friendly to the United States,"[17] and the memorandum accordingly directs commanders to use "information available at the time" to ensure that the recipient fits that qualification.[18] For example, *ex gratia* payments would not be offered to civilians in areas where the population "is in a state of armed conflict or war against the United States."[19] Moreover, the interim regulations note that the principal goal of *ex gratia* payments is to "maintain friendly relations with and the support of local populations where U.S. forces are operating" rather than to serve as a humanitarian tool to help the U.S. military recognize the inevitable loss of life in armed conflict.[20] In deciding whether to offer *ex gratia* payments, commanders are encouraged to consider, among other factors, "mission objectives" and "whether an offer of an

---

[16] U.S. Under Secretary of Defense for Policy, 2020, p. 2.

[17] Pub. L. 116-92, 2019.

[18] U.S. Under Secretary of Defense for Policy, 2020, p. 5.

[19] U.S. Under Secretary of Defense for Policy, 2020, p. 5.

[20] U.S. Under Secretary of Defense for Policy, 2020, p. 1.

ex gratia payment will materially help obtain and maintain friendly relations with . . . local populations where U.S. forces are operating."[21]

The inclusion of this language in Section 1213 and the interim regulations creates concern among civil society organizations that DoD's *ex gratia* payment policy will be disconnected from potential scenarios of future warfare. In fact, the interim regulations state that "*ex gratia* payments may be rare during conventional combat operations," although "commanders may decide to use such payments more frequently in other types of military operations, such as in counterinsurgency or stability operations."[22] As currently written, it is not clear whether commanders operating in contexts of great-power conflict—which are more likely to resemble conventional operations rather than COIN or stability operations—should consider condolence payments as an appropriate response in the wake of unintended incidents of civilian harm. As currently drafted, the interim regulations could impose further barriers on the U.S. forces' disbursement of condolences in response to civilian-harm incidents, such as those in the EUCOM and INDOPACOM AORs, where entire populations may be deemed "unfriendly."[23]

A comparison of recent trends in condolence payments to victims of civilian harm across recent U.S. theaters of operation illustrates how different approaches to combat have already affected the provision of condolences. Condolence payments were seen as a critical component of COIN operations in Afghanistan and Iraq, which relied heavily on major ground operations. During OIR, however, and the associated operational shift prioritizing airpower over ground operations, condolence payments have been largely absent.[24] This has caused significant concern by third-party observers, who estimate that the United States would disburse fewer *ex gratia* payments in the context of future high-intensity conflicts that may prioritize airpower and other assets over ground forces.

DoD's Interim Regulations Lack Sufficient Transparency Around the Determination and Disbursement of *Ex Gratia* Payments

DoD's memorandum on condolence payments lacks sufficient transparency and detail around the determination and disbursement of such payments, which has led to a perception among some critics that payments are not always fair. For example, DoD records show that the U.S. military made approximately $2 million in condolence payments in Afghanistan from 2015 to 2019, but there has been significant fluctua-

---

[21] U.S. Under Secretary of Defense for Policy, 2020, pp. 3–4.

[22] U.S. Under Secretary of Defense for Policy, 2020, p. 4.

[23] NGO representative, interview with the authors, September 2020.

[24] According to our research and interviews with NGO representatives, the United States made one condolence payment to victims in Syria as a result of a January 2019 operation. See also Azmat Khan and Anand Gopal, "The Uncounted," *New York Times Magazine*, November 16, 2017; and Andrea Prasow, "Civilian Casualties: A Case for U.S. Condolence Payments in Syria," *Just Security*, January 6, 2020.

tion across years, and individual sums have drastically varied. As shown in Figure 4.2, condolence payments over that period ranged from $131 in 2019 to $40,000 in 2017. Other details, such as the location of payments, circumstances under which they were made, and the number of individuals across which payments were divided, are also missing from data releases. Our interviews with civil society organizations and former U.S. Army staff judge advocates highlighted that the June 2020 interim regulations around *ex gratia* payments should go further than providing guidance on authorities to approve different payment amounts. As currently written, the regulations leave too much room for units to come to different conclusions when deciding how to provide condolences to harmed civilians and do not allay concerns around the wide discrepancies that exist across payment amounts.[25]

DoD's Interim Regulations Are Just Part of What Should Be a More Comprehensive Response Policy That Addresses All Civilian-Harm Response Options

Finally, because the interim regulations in the memorandum were intended as implementation guidance for Section 1213, which focused only on payments, DoD lacks guidance on the full list of complementary response options that U.S. military commanders have at their disposal to acknowledge harm and provide condolences after civilian-harm incidents. Final guidance on civilian-harm response should be more comprehensive and address a fuller suite of response options. Our interviews with U.S. military commanders with experience in the CENTCOM AOR highlighted the important role that U.S. military responses beyond payments can play in building relationships with local populations. For example, commanders of tactical units operating in Afghanistan during Operation Enduring Freedom and in Iraq during Operation Iraq Freedom stressed that interacting with the local population sometimes paid greater dividends than dispensing condolence payments would have. Ground units deployed to both conflicts said that establishing rapport with local civilians after a civilian-harm incident enhanced the credibility of U.S. forces operating in the area, which was critical to accomplishing subsequent objectives. In addition, NGOs active on the ground developed relationships with civilians, which helped fill gaps in military units' ability to identify and report on civilian-harm incidents, as well as respond to them in a way that meets civilian needs in culturally specific ways.[26] Representatives from civil society organizations who we interviewed as part of this study suggested that, in the aftermath of a civilian casualty incident, the baseline response should be an acknowledgment that harm occurred; in addition, there should be a policy that provides options for commanders to select from a variety of tools designed to accommodate victims' needs.[27]

---

[25] Former U.S. Army staff judge advocate, interview with the authors, September 2020.

[26] U.S. Marine Corps tactical ground units, interview with the authors, March 2020, April 2020.

[27] NGO representative, interview with the authors, September 2020.

Conclusion

DoD's interim regulations on *ex gratia* payments are a step in the right direction in providing some level of standardization for civilian-harm response. However, our research casts doubt on the extent to which a response policy explicitly framed around maintaining the support of local populations where U.S. forces are operating and limited to providing condolences to those deemed friendly to the United States can be applicable to all potential future conflicts. DoD's new guidance improves consistency and transparency—for example, through maximum limits on individual payments and clearer procedures requiring commanders to document the circumstances related to a civilian-harm incident. Further improvements are needed, however, around the types of details that are released about condolence payments and the full list of response options available to commanders in the wake of civilian-harm incidents.

CHAPTER FIVE

DoD Resourcing and Structure to Address Civilian Harm

There is significant variation in how U.S. combatant commands and other DoD components are structured and resourced to address civilian-harm issues. However, just as the GCCs routinely prepare to conduct military operations and therefore have planning and fires cells available, they also must be prepared to respond when operations result in civilian harm, particularly by having available personnel who are skilled in addressing such issues. The military services also play an important role in organizing, training, and equipping their forces to support these missions.

In the first section of this chapter, we outline the GCCs' current resourcing and structures for addressing civilian harm, including the current staffing and expertise at DoD's three CIVCAS cells.[1] We also briefly examine other DoD components, including OSD, the Joint Staff, the military services, U.S. Special Operations Command (SOCOM), and the defense intelligence enterprise. In the second section of this chapter, we present our key findings in this area. Additional information about GCC procedures is available in the online appendix.

Geographic Combatant Commands

U.S. Central Command

CENTCOM headquarters does not have a dedicated CIVCAS cell; the CIVCAS cells in CENTCOM's area of operations sit at the CJTF-OIR and RS headquarters levels. The civilian casualty portfolio at CENTCOM is a collateral (i.e., additional, subordinate) duty for personnel that work in that area. That CENTCOM does not have dedicated staff or a permanent body to assess and learn from civilian-harm incidents is surprising, given the breadth and pace of U.S. military operations in this single region in recent decades.

A CENTCOM Operations Directorate (J3) joint fires element officer (in addition to broader responsibilities that are not related to civilian casualty issues) receives

---

[1] We did not assess U.S. Northern Command, given that its AOR includes only three foreign countries: Canada, Mexico, and the Bahamas.

and manages CENTCOM's responses to civilian casualty inquiries that are not handled by the CJTF-OIR CIVCAS cell or the RS Civilian Casualty Mitigation Team (CCMT).[2] The officer coordinates with representatives from legal, public affairs, or CJTF-OIR or RS, as well as with coalition senior national representatives, as the situation requires.[3] The joint fires element officer also communicates with the CJTF-OIR and RS CIVCAS cells, providing support on archived data requests, congressional notifications and reports, and AR 15-6 investigations, among other activities.[4] And the officer is responsible for conducting civilian-harm assessments for operations occurring in regions without an active CIVCAS cell at a subordinate operational headquarters, such as a JTF.

CENTCOM headquarters may be required to take on additional duties as the number of U.S forces and operations decrease in Afghanistan, Iraq, and Syria and the OIR and RS CIVCAS cells wind down. For example, it will be important to transfer civilian harm–related data, including historical assessments and all supporting operational information, from overseas back to CENTCOM headquarters in Tampa, Florida, so that the information can be accessed for future analysis and any potential reopening of cases. When we broached the topic with CENTCOM officials, they were unaware of any discussions or timelines to transfer civilian-harm duties and data from CJTF-OIR and RS to Tampa, noting that they were not "sure if a withdrawal plan would go to the level of the . . . CIVCAS cell."[5]

A variety of options exist for CENTCOM to engage with external organizations. For example, CENTCOM could produce public-facing websites and public reports; host roundtables with OSD, the Joint Staff, and GCCs; and communicate with NGOs via email.[6] These multiple entry points can complicate engagement and the sharing of information. Indeed, with its current structure and processes, CENTCOM does not appear to have a standardized way of engaging with NGOs or external groups on civilian-harm issues. For example, some CENTCOM officials refused to engage with one particular NGO for a period of time and told us that they would engage the NGO only in group settings.[7] At the same time, NGO personnel reported having some fruitful dialogues with CIVCAS cells at subordinate operational headquarters. The absence of a clear process for engagement creates confusion and generates ill will on both sides. One former general officer interviewed for this report noted that, even if CENTCOM

---

2   The CCMT was called a CIVCAS cell until 2011.

3   CENTCOM military official, email correspondence with the authors, April 2020; and CENTCOM, "RAND Study Responses JFE," Microsoft Word document with responses to author questions, May 2020.

4   CENTCOM military official, email correspondence with the authors, June 2020.

5   CENTCOM military official, email correspondence with the authors, October 2020.

6   CENTCOM military official, email correspondence with the authors, December 2020.

7   NGO officials, interview with the authors, December 2020.

had a formal process or personnel for such activities, CENTCOM "staff do not likely have the expertise to engage substantively on this topic. By design, this expertise is at components and JTFs."[8] Instead, CENTCOM's role should be to set the forum, support the engagement, and integrate the expertise from components and JTFs.

Operation Inherent Resolve

CJTF-OIR maintains a CIVCAS cell of approximately three people. The cell is responsible for civilian casualty assessments in CJTF-OIR's operating area. The cell, along with OIR public affairs, produces a monthly OIR civilian casualty report that is publicly available on the CJTF-OIR and CENTCOM websites.[9] According to CENTCOM, billets for the CIVCAS cell are coded to request members with appropriate operational expertise—for example, in field artillery, infantry, joint fires, and intelligence or operational analysis.[10] However, we interviewed one former CIVCAS cell member who did not have any of these operational skills.[11] As of October 2020, the cell had three members: a field artillery officer, an infantryman, and an intelligence analyst, all of whom perform additional duties for their organization.[12] Our discussions with numerous officials involved with CIVCAS cells indicated that people assigned to these positions often did not have expertise or skills relating to civilian-harm issues. Moreover, CIVCAS cell members at CJTF-OIR (along with their counterparts for RS, discussed next) did not receive formal training on assessing or responding to civilian harm prior to or during their deployment. There is a "constant relearning" that occurs, and no "legacy knowledge" on civilian-harm issues exists within the cells.[13]

Resolute Support

The CCMT at RS is responsible for tracking civilian casualties, assessing the credibility of civilian-harm reports, and mentoring the Government of Afghanistan and the Afghan National Defense and Security Forces to help them develop and maintain a credible and sustainable capability to mitigate Afghan-caused civilian harm.[14]

The RS CCMT is currently billeted for five people, including two members from North Atlantic Treaty Organization countries. As of October 2020, the team com-

---

8 Former general officer, interview with the authors, December 2020.

9 CJTF-OIR official, interview with the authors, May 2020. See CJTF-OIR, "CIVCAS Releases," webpage, undated-a.

10 CENTCOM and CJTF-OIR officials, interview with the authors, June 2020.

11 Former CJTF-OIR official, interview with the authors, May 2020.

12 CJTF-OIR military official, email correspondence with the authors, October 2020.

13 CENTCOM official, interview with the authors, June 2020.

14 Operation Resolute Support Civilian Casualty Mitigation Team, "RAND CIVCAS Study – RS Response as of 28 April," Microsoft Word document provided to the authors, April 2020; and U.S. Forces Afghanistan, "Memorandum for Record USFOR-A RAND Response," Microsoft Word document provided to the authors, USFOR-A-OPS-J5-CCMT, October 20, 2020.

prised three U.S. Army officers, a Belgian noncommissioned officer, and a civilian from the Alliance.[15] The CCMT's structure has fluctuated over time, at times with junior officers filling billets slated for more-senior officers. For example, in summer 2020, the chief of the CCMT, a Marine Corps captain (O-3), was filling a lieutenant colonel (O-5) billet.[16] Since the CCMT's inception in 2008, the organization responsible for it has changed and was located under various elements of CENTCOM J3 and the deputy chief of staff for operations. As of March 2020, CENTCOM's Strategy and Plans Directorate (J5) assumed responsibility for the CCMT, where it continues to sit as a section of the Afghan Assessments Group.[17]

U.S. Africa Command

AFRICOM's Operations Directorate (J3) oversees the assessment of reports of potential civilian casualties. The J3's Fires and Effects Branch manages the assessment process, with input from the Office of Legal Counsel. The CIVCAS cell also includes personnel from the Intelligence Directorate (J2). Although AFRICOM's Office of Public Affairs and Communication plays a role in assessing reported civilian casualties, public affairs officers are not part of the CIVCAS cell.[18]

Similar to the circumstances in CENTCOM, the assessment of civilian casualty reports is a collateral duty for members of the AFRICOM CIVCAS cell.[19] Within AFRICOM, the CIVCAS cell is viewed as an "assignment that no one wants to handle."[20] Despite this perception, the CIVCAS cell performs a vital function, and its members must be "fully committed to the job."[21] Similar to CENTCOM, AFRICOM has no standardized process for engaging external groups, and many engagements are ad hoc and based on personal relationships. For example, interviewees stated that an NGO might have a dialogue with the CIVCAS cell, but such a dialogue is later denied to another NGO conducting a similar review or investigation.[22] Moreover, one NGO official reported that AFRICOM officials do not necessarily speak with one voice on civilian casualty issues; for example, headquarters elements are hesitant to speak on behalf of subordinate elements of the command.[23]

---

[15] U.S. Forces Afghanistan, 2020.

[16] RS official, interview with the authors, May 2020.

[17] RS Civilian Casualty Mitigation Team, 2020; U.S. Forces Afghanistan, 2020.

[18] AFRICOM official, interview with the authors, April 2020.

[19] AFRICOM military official, interview with the authors, April 2020, May 2020.

[20] AFRICOM official, interview with the authors, April 2020.

[21] AFRICOM official, interview with the authors, April 2020.

[22] NGO officials, interview with the authors, December 2020.

[23] NGO officials, interview with the authors, December 2020.

Individuals we interviewed suggested that AFRICOM should have a standalone CIVCAS cell with staff dedicated to those duties only. This would permit the members of the cell to be "100 percent focused on [assessing] potential [civilian casualty] reports."[24] One official we spoke with recommended that AFRICOM should have "two dedicated action officers who just manage [civilian casualties] from cradle to grave."[25] Others suggested that a standalone cell should have five or six members.[26] At present, the CIVCAS cell is housed within the Directorate of Operations and Cyber, which means that, from the perspective of human rights NGOs, the "same people [are] carrying out the strikes and assessing them."[27] The creation of a standalone CIVCAS cell would underscore its independence and highlight AFRICOM's commitment to transparency.

In addition, the CIVCAS cell would benefit from a more formalized onboarding process for new members, who are "just thrown into the deep end." One official noted that additional training would have the added benefit of improving public trust in the command's work.[28]

Furthermore, AFRICOM officials indicated that, if there was an "uptick in incidents," the CIVCAS cell's existing processes would be "too labor-intensive" at current staffing levels.[29] The cell would "be underwater."[30] Whenever a strike is conducted, one official explained, military personnel "expect there to be an allegation" of civilian casualties, which means that the full assessment process must be initiated and carried out.[31]

U.S. European Command

EUCOM does not maintain a standing cell dedicated to responding to potential civilian casualty reports, and the command is waiting for the finalization of DoD's forthcoming policy guidance before developing its own policy. Nevertheless, our research suggests that operators and planners assigned to this theater are thinking about the issue. Specifically, interviewees stated that investigations in response to reports of potential civilian harm would likely proceed in accordance with the military's commander-directed investigation processes, such as those outlined in AR 15-6 or Army in Europe

[24] AFRICOM military official, interview with the authors, April 2020.

[25] AFRICOM official, interview with the authors, April 2020.

[26] AFRICOM civilian official, interview with the authors, April 2020; AFRICOM military official, interview with the authors, April 2020.

[27] AFRICOM civilian official, interview with the authors, April 2020.

[28] AFRICOM official, interview with the authors, April 2020.

[29] AFRICOM official, interview with the authors, April 2020.

[30] AFRICOM civilian official, interview with the authors, April 2020.

[31] AFRICOM military official, interview with the authors, April 2020.

Regulation 27-8.[32] In terms of personnel, staff from EUCOM's Operations Directorate (J3) and staff judge advocates assigned to the command are involved in conversations about revised guidance.

EUCOM staff are eager to ensure that a new DoD Instruction on civilian casualty policy accounts for the types of conflict that may be encountered in the AOR in the future—namely, high-intensity conflict with a near-peer adversary. Currently, there is concern among staff that extant DoD policies around responding to civilian-harm incidents cannot apply to this type of conflict. One interviewee, for example, stated that past drafts of the policy seemed primarily focused on intra-state conflicts: "In a state versus state conflict, the requirements to investigate all reports would be implacable and invite numerous fraudulent reports by adversaries."[33] EUCOM officials were also concerned that conflicts between peer adversaries could yield an overwhelming number of civilian casualty allegations that prevent timely investigations.[34] And officials expressed doubt over the functionality of a web portal (like AFRICOM's) to report civilian casualty incidents: "Name your [adversary] country and they can create a bot to flood [the web portal]."[35]

In short, there are concerns among EUCOM staff that a policy specifying the same set of requirements across all combatant commands would open DoD up to even more criticism when the scale of certain types of conflicts—specifically, conventional warfare against a near-peer adversary—could preclude the investigation of every single allegation. Although the civilian casualty challenges of high-intensity combat may seem overwhelming, additional resourcing and staffing dedicated to preparing for these problems could prove beneficial, particularly if they can improve the dialogue among GCCs, OSD, the Joint Staff, and the military services.

U.S. Indo-Pacific Command

Due to a lack of active combat operations, INDOPACOM, like EUCOM, does not have a standing cell to assess and investigate potential civilian casualty reports.[36] As of summer 2020, INDOPACOM's Command, Control, Communications, and Cyber Directorate (J6), legal staff, and the Center for Excellence in Disaster Management and Humanitarian Assistance (CFE-DM) split responsibility over civilian casualty planning, which is limited to the development of no-strike lists and collateral damage estimation considerations. CFE-DM plays an advisory role in the development of command-specific policies around civilian casualties and represents the command in

---

32 EUCOM official, interview with the authors, April 2020.

33 EUCOM official, interview with the authors, April 2020.

34 EUCOM official, interview with the authors, April 2020.

35 EUCOM official, interview with the authors, April 2020.

36 INDOPACOM official, interview with the authors, April 2020.

OSD civilian casualty working group discussions.[37] This arrangement was still evolving as of January 2021. Otherwise, the command itself remains only partially organized and resourced to assess and report on civilian harm. In particular, planning for civilian casualties is a collateral duty, although INDOPACOM plans to formally appoint staff to more-specific roles in the future. Prior to the aforementioned arrangement involving CFE-DM, INDOPACOM's Future Operations Division, Operations Directorate (J355) was responsible for issues related to civilian casualties.[38]

Absent the finalized DoD policy around assessing and investigating civilian harm, INDOPACOM has largely relied on previously published DoD and Joint Staff guidance and processes for assessing, investigating, and responding to civilian casualty allegations. For example, INDOPACOM would leverage the AR 15-6 process in the case of a civilian casualty incident in its region. INDOPACOM also maintains preliminary plans to stand up an ad hoc working group—with representatives from at least legal and joint fires headquarters elements—to handle reports of civilian harm. The idea would be to regularly assess the size and status of this working group to support the pace of combat operations. INDOPACOM also plans to maintain civilian casualty mitigation cells at subordinate component commands, JTFs, or both to support assessment and investigation in the event of combat operations.[39]

In June 2020, INDOPACOM drafted a preliminary command policy letter and associated standard operating procedures on civilian harm.[40] According to our interviews with command representatives, the letter (still in draft form as of January 2021) focuses exclusively on issues related to reporting and recording civilian-harm incidents and does not consider procedures or guidance around mitigating harm. There is also a lack of clarity around communication and coordination with international organizations, such as the United Nations, and civil society organizations.[41]

The draft guidance addresses investigation criteria and states the intent to make the results of all investigations public, although how INDOPACOM would do so is not specified. The command also intends to maintain a database and incident-tracking system to record incidents of civilian harm incurred in its AOR. According to our interviews, INDOPACOM is waiting to finalize its own guidance until DoD releases its finalized guidance.[42] As with EUCOM, additional resourcing and staffing dedicated

---

[37] INDOPACOM official, interview with the authors, October 2020.

[38] INDOPACOM official, email correspondence with the authors, September 2020.

[39] INDOPACOM official, interview with the authors, April 2020.

[40] We requested a copy of the letter and the standard operating procedures, which are not publicly available, but had not received them as of this writing in early 2021.

[41] INDOPACOM official, interview with the authors, October 2020.

[42] INDOPACOM official, interview with the authors, October 2020.

to civilian-harm issues might improve INDOPACOM's preparedness for the immense challenges of high-intensity combat until the draft guidance becomes finalized.

U.S. Southern Command

Because of the low probability of U.S. combat operations in Latin America or the Caribbean, SOUTHCOM has neither personnel dedicated to addressing civilian casualties nor a standing CIVCAS cell. Its Human Rights Office, however, deals with issues that fall under the broad scope of civilian protection. SOUTHCOM's civilian deputy to the commander and foreign policy adviser is responsible for overseeing human rights initiatives, and at the end of 2020, the Human Rights Office was undergoing a transition from three to six full-time civilian staff. Funding for the command's Human Rights Initiative (described in detail in the online appendix), is commander-driven and comes entirely from within the command. Most of the funding goes toward organizing exchanges of information among subject-matter experts and conferences focused on human rights in the region.[43] Although funding constraints limit the extent to which SOUTHCOM's Human Rights Office can fully engage partner countries (for example, it does not conduct or support training with partner-nation militaries), the self-funded structure grants the office a certain level of agility. Nevertheless, rolling SOUTHCOM's Human Rights Initiative into a larger, DoD-managed and -funded initiative around civilian protection could introduce significant advantages, particularly by providing access to more-consistent funding streams. In other words, although SOUTHCOM would play a minimal role in civilian casualty assessments, it would play a more prominent role in a DoD-wide approach to civilian protection that incorporated a variety of issues, such as civilian harm, human rights, mass-atrocity prevention, and women's role in peace and security.

Other DoD Components

Office of the Secretary of Defense

The Deputy Under Secretary of Defense for Policy is the DoD civilian official responsible for developing, coordinating, and overseeing compliance with DoD's policy relating to civilian casualties. This position sits within OSD, and its day-to-day responsibilities fall to the Deputy Assistant Secretary of Defense for Stability and Humanitarian Affairs. One permanent and one temporary staff member spend the majority of their time on civilian casualty policy issues. OSD's Office of the General Counsel also has two legal counsels who spend a portion of their time on civilian casualty issues.

The Office of the Under Secretary of Defense for Policy engages other OSD organizations—for example, those overseen by the Under Secretaries of Defense for

---

[43] SOUTHCOM official, interview with the authors, October 2020.

Intelligence and Security, Research and Engineering, Acquisition and Sustainment, Comptroller, and Personnel and Readiness—on certain civilian casualty policy issues. However, these organizations do not have staff officially tasked to support these issues, resulting in sporadic and reactive involvement. The Defense Security Cooperation Agency has one permanent staff member who works on policies relating to the civilian casualty practices of foreign military partners, often in coordination with the Office of the Under Secretary of Defense for Policy and the Department of State, and one additional staff member who supports that portfolio.

We found that a lack of formal written guidance, insufficient staffing, and—with the exception of the Office of the Under Secretary of Defense for Policy and General Counsel divisions—inconsistent leadership attention limited the impact of the individuals in these organizations dedicated to effective civilian casualty policies. When published, DoD's policy on civilian-harm mitigation and civilian casualty response will be a critical step forward in formally prescribing civilian casualty roles and responsibilities across DoD and elaborating on its procedures for assessing, investigating, and responding to civilian-harm incidents.

Joint Staff

The Joint Staff's Strategy, Plans, and Policy Directorate (J5) has one military officer (an O-5, which is the lieutenant colonel or commander level) responsible for supporting the Chairman of the Joint Chiefs of Staff on civilian casualty issues. This officer serves as an important bridge between the Pentagon's civilian leadership and U.S. military leaders in the armed services and combatant commands. However, because the officer in this position is rotated every two to three years and receives no formal civilian casualty training, it is difficult to maintain institutional knowledge on DoD's complex civilian casualty policies and procedures in the Joint Staff. This problem is not necessarily unique to civilian casualties, as almost all Joint Staff positions have the same issue.

Other Joint Staff directorates are relevant but have been less actively engaged on these issues. For example, the Targeting Doctrine and Policy branch of the Intelligence (J2) and Operations (J3) Directorates could issue guidance that puts greater emphasis on civilian protection in the targeting cycle and operational planning. The Joint Force Development Directorate (J7) could engage by developing doctrine and setting requirements for analysis and training. For example, the J7 has a staff officer responsible for overseeing training related to the issue of women's role in peace and security at multiple levels across DoD.[44]

---

[44] DoD officials, interview with the authors, January 2021.

Military Services

The Army, Navy, Air Force, and Marine Corps are responsible for organizing, training, and equipping U.S. military forces, and this responsibility includes preparing the joint force to mitigate and respond to civilian harm. Although GCCs and other DoD components support these preparations in various ways, the military services ultimately play the lead role in, for example, developing doctrine and operating concepts; educating, training, and exercising units and personnel; analyzing trends and institutionalizing lessons from ground, maritime, and air domain perspectives; identifying relevant technologies; and acquiring capabilities to improve situational awareness of the operational environment, including tools that can integrate information from various sources, such as ISR feeds and weapon systems.

To be sure, we found that the military services already incorporate civilian-harm mitigation and response issues into their organize, train, and equip responsibilities, particularly as part of broader efforts to ensure adherence to the law of war. But they are sprawling organizations, and it can be difficult to find central interlocutors to discuss these issues in a comprehensive, detailed way. More could be done to give the services a stronger voice at the headquarters level so that they can ensure they are sufficiently engaged on these issues and responding adequately to the demand signals from OSD, the Joint Staff, and the GCCs. The services could also play a stronger role through their professional military education responsibilities.

For example, the military services operate several schools that prepare their personnel to conduct strategic and operational planning and that provide critical thinking skills to solve the military's most-challenging problems. DoD's advanced planning schools could strengthen the focus of their curricula to include real-world examples of civilian-harm assessments and investigations to help students understand the root causes of civilian harm, possible solutions,[45] and their implications.[46] Service schools could also build on existing resources, such as the National Defense University's Burning Sands wargame, which challenges players to complete a military mission while addressing civilian-harm issues.[47]

U.S. Special Operations Command

As a force provider, SOCOM does not have operational control of special operations forces (SOF) elements. When those forces deploy and conduct operations, they report to the relevant GCC and follow its processes for civilian casualty assessments. For exam-

---

[45] DoD often analyzes solutions across the spectrum of DOTMLPF-P: doctrine, organization, training, materiel, leadership and education, personnel, facilities, and policy.

[46] DoD's advanced planning schools include the Army's School of Advanced Military Studies, the Air Force's School of Advanced Air and Space Studies, the Navy's Maritime Advanced Warfighting School, and the Joint Staff's Joint Advanced Warfighting School.

[47] Thomas J. Gordon IV, Adam Oler, Laurie Blank, and Jill Goldenziel, "Lawyers, Guns, and Twitter: Wargamig the Role of Law in War," *War on the Rocks*, February 2, 2021.

ple, for reports of potential civilian casualties during OIR, the CJTF-OIR CIVCAS cell tasked the unit that acted as the target engagement authority for the strike with completing the CCAR, which could include OIR's Special Operations Joint Task Force and associated SOF elements in the area of operations.[48] Despite the lack of headquarters responsibilities related to civilian casualty assessments and reporting, the SOCOM commander is often copied on CCARs and SOF units' post-deployment after-action reports. Through review of these documents, SOCOM identifies and implements lessons learned to improve SOF support to GCC missions and goals.[49]

However, SOCOM also performs missions of a functional combatant command and conducts operations via a subordinate JTF. Given that role and the sustained SOF operations over the past two decades, some SOF elements have developed internal processes for tracking, assessing, and learning from civilian casualties, which over time have informed GCC processes and methodologies. For example, SOF keep extremely detailed records of their strikes and relevant associated information, including the result of the strike, in a database. According to a SOF commander, these logs were shared as a best practice across the CENTCOM theater during OIR.[50] SOF then used these strike logs to design a strike simulation at the Air Force Research Laboratory. The simulation enabled SOF to "stare down at terrain that exactly replicated Syria, in a computer simulation projected on screens just as it would be in a tactical command center."[51] The simulation contained ISIS fighters, civilians, and unknown personnel and was designed to present SOF with the same tactical dilemmas they would face once they deployed, including civilian casualty issues.

Defense Intelligence Enterprise

The defense intelligence enterprise's strategic organizations—including the Defense Intelligence Agency, the National Geospatial-Intelligence Agency (NGA), and the Office of the Under Secretary of Defense for Intelligence and Security—play no active role in operational civilian casualty assessments and therefore have no people dedicated to the effort.[52] That said, intelligence does play a role in civilian-harm issues more generally. In Chapter Two, we discussed the role that intelligence plays in target development, collateral damage estimation or assessment, and battle damage assessment. The Defense Intelligence Agency maintains the databases required to support those functions: the Modernized Integrated Database and its eventual replacement, the Machine-

---

[48] SOCOM civilian official, interview with the authors, December 2020.

[49] SOCOM civilian official, interview with the authors, December 2020.

[50] SOF commander, interview with the authors, January 2021.

[51] SOF commander, interview with the authors, January 2021.

[52] Defense intelligence official, interview with the authors, July 2020.

Assisted Analytic Rapid-Repository System.[53] The agency also reviews GCCs' deliberate target development efforts. However, except in specific circumstances, the agency is not involved in battle damage assessment analysis, unless it is to assess the functionality of a holistic military system. Otherwise, the GCCs maintain responsibilities for conducting battle damage assessments. NGA additionally plays a role in understanding the human terrain and targeting development efforts. Through its oversight of Oak Ridge National Laboratory's population density tables and LandScan, tools that estimate local population levels and locations, NGA supports deliberate target development.[54] Like the Defense Intelligence Agency, NGA also reviews GCCs' deliberate target development efforts.

Key Findings: DoD Resourcing and Structure for Addressing Civilian Harm

Geographic Combatant Commands and Other DoD Components Do Not Have Sufficient Dedicated, Trained Personnel for Civilian-Harm Issues

The combatant commands—even those engaged in active armed conflicts—do not have personnel whose full-time portfolios focus exclusively on civilian harm. The RS mission and CJTF-OIR have dedicated CIVCAS cells, but the personnel assigned to these cells do not receive pre-deployment training on the duties that they will be expected to perform beyond general DoD law of war training. Although billets for the cells are typically coded to ensure that the cells include members with appropriate operational expertise—for instance, field artillery, infantry, joint fires, and intelligence analysis—there is no standardized or formal training for cell members prior to their arrival at post.[55] The lack of training or standards requires CIVCAS cell personnel to learn informally from their predecessors or on the job. Some CIVCAS cell personnel also reported receiving insufficient guidance on their duties and responsibilities. According to one U.S. operator, the cell could have benefited from additional guidance on "how deep it should dig into each allegation, how much effort it should put into verifying the reliability of a source, and what to do if there were conflicting

---

[53] The Modernized Integrated Database is the national-level repository for the general military intelligence available to the entire DoD Intelligence Information System community and to tactical units. Entity-level target development data for all target types are included in the database and accessed by intelligence analysts and targeting professionals who are conducting target development assessments and collateral damage estimations or building a no-strike list or restricted target list. See CJCSI 3370.01B, *Target Development Standards*, Washington, D.C.: Joint Chiefs of Staff, May 6, 2016, Not available to the general public.

[54] The population density tables support the requirement for combatant commands to incorporate demographic data in order to support operational planning and execution, as stated in CJCSI 3160.01C and CJCSI 3370.01B (Oak Ridge National Laboratory, "Population Density Tables," presentation, June 2020).

[55] Operational command staff, interview with the authors, June 2020; CENTCOM officials, interview with the authors, May 2020; DoD official, interview with the authors, October 2020.

cases."[56] CENTCOM and AFRICOM would both benefit from more people with more expertise focusing on civilian-harm issues, particularly assessments. EUCOM and INDOPACOM are not involved in combat operations, but, given that they maintain fires cells and conduct extensive planning for potential conflicts, they also need to be ready to account for civilian harm that may result from those conflicts. Even SOUTHCOM, which has far less potential for overseeing U.S. combat operations, would benefit from additional personnel and resources dedicated to civilian protection, including for its work with partner militaries.

OSD and Joint Staff officials face similar challenges, lacking sufficient dedicated staff and negligible training. These limitations drive officials to move from crisis to crisis with insufficient time to be proactive and strategic or to use more-extensive analysis in support of their oversight efforts. Some parts of OSD have failed to leverage the expertise and resources of their organizations. Lack of assigned staff and leadership attention has constrained the exploration of technology, acquisition, data management, and other solutions to civilian casualty challenges.

Because of their large size and wide scope of responsibilities, it is difficult to judge whether the military services are adequately resourced to address civilian-harm issues. Their roles, however, were rarely mentioned during the dozens of discussions we held across DoD, and some stakeholders had trouble identifying officials within the services who have significant responsibilities for civilian-harm issues from an institutional perspective. Thus, it seems that the military services could play a more proactive, visible role in organizing, training, and equipping their forces to better address civilian-harm risks and responses.

Considering the frequent criticisms we heard about inadequate training, each service would likely also benefit from developing more-robust training programs. Because civilian-harm issues are often embedded as part of other topics and activities, they may suffer from a lack of higher-level coordination and dedicated attention that would make them more prominent in the minds of leaders, planners, and operators. There may also be room for improved coordination across the joint force and with other DoD components so that different organizations can leverage each other's activities, share best practices, and identify efficiencies.

These shortfalls in personnel with sufficient expertise in civilian-harm issues were exacerbated by the lack of a central focal point within DoD to proactively promote collaboration and learning across the broad variety of civilian protection activities undertaken by DoD, including not only civilian-harm issues but also such topics as human rights and mass-atrocity prevention. OSD and Joint Staff officials—some of whom themselves lack expertise related to civilian protection issues—have oversight responsibilities that often prove overwhelming. Although larger staffs with more relevant experience and training would certainly help, their focus on supporting senior DoD leaders

---

[56] Operational command staff, interview with the authors, June 2020.

will always limit the extent to which they can serve as a catalyst for improvements at the operational and tactical levels. A DoD organization that could play the role of catalyst was one of the most-important gaps we found in our research.

Finally, as DoD officials work to implement their new policy instruction on civilian-harm issues, it will be important to discuss the balance between providing combatant commands and military services with flexibility while also developing common standards. OSD and the Joint Staff would benefit from issuing a policy implementation roadmap that provides clear, consistent guidance and a baseline of standardized requirements that meet the expectations of DoD's most-senior leaders, Congress, and the American people.

DoD Is Not Organized to Monitor and Analyze Civilian Casualty Trends and Patterns over Time

The CIVCAS cells and the CCAR process have helped ensure that each report of a civilian casualty is assessed by the U.S. military. Although this is an improvement in the accountability and transparency of U.S. military operations, the individual tracking of civilian-harm incidents does not necessarily mean that the U.S. military is learning lessons from those incidents. The role of the CIVCAS cells is to receive reports, gather supporting information, and make an assessment based on the information collected. Neither the cells nor any other parts of DoD have the personnel or capability to analyze civilian casualty data, from both internal and external sources, in a meaningful way over time.

Commands Lack Clear Processes for Assuming Control of Civilian Casualty Data and Responsibilities When Active Operations Cease

Commands do not have a process to ensure that civilian casualty data are archived and responsibilities are transferred at the end of major operations. CENTCOM, as a command whose number of active operations conducted by U.S. forces is decreasing and whose operational headquarters is similarly downsizing, is currently the principal illustration of this problem. As of January 2021, CJTF-OIR and RS headquarters remained established and active, and thus they "maintain the authority and requirement to manage and assess reports of civilian casualties."[57] According to our research, CENTCOM headquarters recognizes that civilian casualty responsibilities will return to Tampa, Florida, but the command has not yet delineated processes or timelines for that movement.[58] As of October 2020, the CJTF-OIR and RS CIVCAS cells had not been included in and were not aware of any discussions related to retrograding

---

[57] CENTCOM military official, email correspondence with the authors, October 2020.

[58] CENTCOM military official, email correspondence with the authors, October 2020.

responsibilities back to CENTCOM.[59] In response to data requested for this study, we found that RS has transferred some, but not all, civilian casualty–related data to CENTCOM, but it is not clear that CENTCOM will be pulling remaining data during the drawdown of forces in Afghanistan.[60] Currently, AFRICOM headquarters and its CIVCAS cell manage the assessment process, because the command lacks CIVCAS cells at subordinate operational commands or JTFs. This setup eliminates the data transfer concerns that CENTCOM faces. However, if the responsibilities do devolve to a subordinate command in the future, AFRICOM would need to consider the processes necessary to establish a subordinate cell and retain critical data.

Conclusion

Our research suggests that DoD is not adequately organized, trained, or equipped to fulfill its current responsibilities for addressing civilian harm. For instance, DoD's CIVCAS cells are often staffed by junior personnel who do not receive formal training on the duties and responsibilities that they will be expected to perform, leaving them to learn on the job with guidance that is often insufficient. EUCOM and INDOPACOM do not have CIVCAS cells or personnel dedicated to civilian casualty issues and are only in the early stages of thinking about how they would assess, investigate, and respond to civilian-harm issues in the event of a conflict. Civilian-harm assessments, investigations, and responses would also benefit from additional staff with the right expertise in other DoD components, particularly OSD, the Joint Staff, and the military services. Finally, DoD is missing structures and capabilities for important activities, such as analyzing and monitoring civilian-harm trends over time and archiving data. The improvements that we identified in the tracking of individual civilian-harm incidents have not necessarily translated into the U.S. military learning lessons from those incidents.

---

[59] CJTF-OIR military official, email correspondence with the authors, October 2020; RS military official, email correspondence with the authors, October 2020.

[60] RS military official, email correspondence with the authors, October 2020.

CHAPTER SIX

Recommendations

In this final chapter of the report, we begin with an overview of the recommendations produced by the 2018 Joint Staff *Civilian Casualty (CIVCAS) Review* and our assessment of their implementation to date. We then provide our own recommendations, based on the congressional guidance provided to us through the FY 2020 NDAA and the broader scope of our study.

Status of the Implementation of Joint Staff Review Recommendations

As discussed in Chapter One, the 2018 Joint Staff review recommended nine steps for DoD to improve its ability to mitigate and account for civilian casualties.[1] In response, OSD and the Joint Staff developed an internal implementation plan, which was signed by then–Secretary of Defense James Mattis, that succeeded in taking some initial steps toward improving DoD's ability to mitigate and respond to civilian casualty incidents. However, we argue that, based on the research presented in this report, DoD still has a long way to go in implementing these recommendations.

Table 6.1 provides our assessment of DoD's progress implementing the recommendations in the Joint Staff review; this assessment is current as of early 2021.

Many of the challenges in implementing these recommendations, as well as those from our research, stem from an overarching requirement for DoD to view civilian-harm issues and their solutions as institutional, not just operational. In her book *Chasing Success: Air Force Efforts to Reduce Civilian Harm*, Sarah Sewall notes that institutional change in the area of civilian harm includes such areas as data collection, learning, analysis, expertise, institutional responsibility, and the evaluation of U.S. success. It involves "internalization within the services that civilian casualty reduction is not something that automatically happens but rather requires dedicated attention: technology, tactics, training, and so forth."[2]

---

[1]   Joint Staff, 2018.

[2]   Sarah Sewall, *Chasing Success: Air Force Efforts to Reduce Civilian Harm*, Maxwell Air Force Base, Ala.: Air Force University Press, 2016, p. 178.

Table 6.1
DoD's Progress Implementing the Recommendations in the Joint Staff Review

Recommendation[a]	Implementation Status	Explanation
1, 2 Clarify guidance and doctrine to address the increased risk of civilian casualties when U.S. forces operate by, with, and through partner forces.	**Not yet implemented.**	There is a lack of clarity over DoD's "by, with, and through" concept and thus the scope of the recommendation.[b] Moreover, there is no clear lead for implementation, given the number of DoD components with a stake in this recommendation, such as the GCCs, SOCOM, the Defense Security Cooperation Agency, and the Office of the Under Secretary Defense for Policy.
3 Invest in tools to assist ground force commanders with situational awareness.	**Not yet implemented.**	DoD has struggled to identify which component owns the responsibilities for overseeing research and acquisition related to civilian harm.
4 Systematically seek out additional sources of information on potential civilian casualties as part of the self-reporting process. These include social media, NGOs, and local sources. Place greater emphasis on civilian casualties as part of the battle damage assessment.	**Substantial implementation progress.** RS updated its procedures in 2020 to conduct inquiries into civilian casualty reports appearing on social media and in news outlets. CJTF-OIR's intelligence analyst conducts social media searches for civilian casualty reports. Analysts in AFRICOM's Joint Operations Center also search open-source media for potential civilian casualty reports, but the task is not required by the center's policy. RS maintains a long-standing relationship with the United Nations Assistance Mission in Afghanistan and the International Committee of the Red Cross, while CJTF-OIR frequently communicates with Airwars on the topic of civilian harm. A new DoD webpage provides information about how to submit information to DoD about civilian casualties that may have resulted from U.S. military operations.[c] AFRICOM has also launched an internet-based mechanism for accepting reports of civilian casualties. The March 2019 version of CJCSI 3162.02, *Methodology for Combat Assessment*, requires, rather than recommends, a combat assessment for target engagements.	Despite the revised CJCSI, we did not find that there has been an additional emphasis on identifying civilian casualties during the combat assessment process.

Table 6.1—Continued

Recommendation[a]	Implementation Status	Explanation
5	Consider standardizing the civilian casualty review process across combatant commands.	**Implementation underway.** CENTCOM, AFRICOM, CJTF-OIR, and RS have their own procedures for civilian casualty reporting and review, although they are similar. Other combatant commands do not have similar procedures.	DoD is working to finalize a DoD Instruction that will standardize procedures across DoD and its components, but the guidance had not yet been released as of this writing.
6	Expand combatant command–level CIVCAS cells to include individuals tasked with reconciling external and U.S. military reports on civilian casualties, as well as coordinating with relevant units to declassify or appropriately release relevant information.	**Partially implemented.** CIVCAS cells have not been expanded in terms of personnel, but part of the duties of the CIVCAS cells are to review external reports on civilian casualties.	
7	The joint force should develop a process for initial assessment reports that broadens the geographic area and time frame of inquiry. The process should provide flexibility to account for contextual and operational differences across AORs. The joint force should also create a range of estimates of civilian casualty numbers and report those estimates (i.e., confirmed, disputed, rejected).	**Not yet implemented.**	The forthcoming DoD Instruction on civilian-harm mitigation and response will provide overarching guidance for reporting civilian harm. DoD is still debating the advantages and disadvantages of using a range of estimates for civilian casualty numbers and had not come to a decision as of this writing.
8	The military should institutionalize civilian casualty investigation processes. This should include sharing best practices in AR 15-6 adjudication and public release, as well as closer engagement with NGOs during the process, where feasible.	**Not yet implemented.**	DoD continues to lack a centralized node capable of compiling lessons learned and best practices from assessments and investigations of civilian harm.

Table 6.1—Continued

Recommendation[a]	Implementation Status	Explanation
9 The joint staff should develop specific guidance, processes, and clarifications of authorities for combatant commands for civilian casualty response (e.g., compensation, explanation, working through partner governments, in-kind offerings, community projects, apologies, clearing of the family name). Such guidance should be informed by particular host-nation customs, laws, and norms.	**Partially implemented.** In June 2020, DoD released a memorandum with interim regulations that focus exclusively on condolence payments. There is no other DoD guidance on a wider variety of responses to civilian harm.	The memorandum reported that these interim regulations will be replaced by a new DoD Instruction or incorporated into an existing DoD Instruction before February 25, 2022.

[a] The recommendations in this column are adapted from Joint Staff, 2018.

[b] "By, with, and through" is common shorthand for how U.S. forces work with allies and partners.

[c] See U.S. Under Secretary of Defense for Policy, "Reporting Civilian Casualties," webpage, undated.

Thus, we recommend that OSD and the Joint Staff update the Secretary of Defense–signed roadmap for implementing the 2018 recommendations, with an emphasis on institutional improvements across the joint force. The roadmap could perhaps be incorporated into a broader OSD-led effort to support implementation of our additional recommendations, which we describe in the remainder of this chapter.

Recommendations for Assessments of Civilian Harm

Expand the Kinds of Information Available for Assessments to Make Them More Robust

The U.S. military's assessments of civilian casualties are important but require improvements. We found that, in conducting civilian casualty assessments, the military is striving to deal with a hard problem—the inherent uncertainty of determining operational outcomes given the fog of war and military capabilities that have stark limitations in certain contexts. Air campaigns in particular have inherent problems detecting civilian harm, and the U.S. military must grapple with these issues. The military is further challenged by the fact that U.S. operational data are not comprehensive, and DoD cannot expect to have a perfect operational picture. Thus, this recommendation, and the two that follow, focus on ensuring that DoD leverages the best possible information—including internal and external data—for assessments.

DoD should ensure that the best possible data are used to identify and assess possible civilian harm. As this report has demonstrated, ISR and FMV are powerful tools but are insufficient when it comes to accurately and completely assessing civilian harm. Although these and other technological tools currently available to the U.S. military are vital resources, they also have limitations. Thus, incorporating lessons from all-source intelligence analysis remains critical. Expanding the kinds of information available for assessments can make them more robust.

DoD can better integrate information on civilian harm from sources outside of the military. For example, the military's assessments should leverage the resources of local reporting to make more-informed decisions about reports of possible civilian harm. In addition, the military should be more transparent about what information is required to report civilian harm (e.g., exact location data and time) and should communicate these details to civilians and NGO actors in conflict areas so that they can collect and provide relevant details when an incident occurs.

There are additional capabilities or tools that the U.S. military can pursue to strengthen its ability to make robust assessments and better understand operational outcomes and decisions. For example, certain mobile apps that rely on blockchain technology to securely upload images or video of civilian-harm incidents with embedded metadata, including geographic location and timestamps to ensure credibility, are particularly promising in this regard.[3] In addition, given the richness of new data sets (such as from social media) and the success of such groups as Bellingcat in correlating satellite imagery with other images, the military could develop tools to support incident reconstructions while also identifying other potential incidents of concern. To illustrate the potential value of these data and tools, Bellingcat analysts convened a workshop in 2019 to reconstruct a set of civilian-harm incidents in Yemen by working with journalists, human rights lawyers, and military experts. In many cases, these reconstructions yielded additional information beyond what was available on record from the Saudi-led coalition. For example, for a 2018 strike on a medical facility, the coalition claimed that the facility lacked red crescent markings, but the Bellingcat-led reconstruction located the facility and found that it was indeed marked.[4] The U.S. military could use this same approach to open-source data to augment its information for assessments. In addition to helping with assessments, this approach would be valuable for the military to use in targeting decisions to strengthen collateral damage estimates and better deconflict humanitarian entities, such as hospitals and essential infrastructure.

Another option that DoD has to expand the information available for assessments is to conduct site visits and witness interviews. As noted in Chapter Two, for the vast majority of incidents of civilian harm in OIR, particularly those in Syria, the United

---

[3] Several emerging mobile app platforms have already deployed this technology in Syria—for example, Sealr.app (Sealr, homepage, undated) and Native.io (Native, "Aid & Development," webpage, undated).

[4] Lewis, 2019b.

States and coalition forces did not use site visits as part of their assessments, partly because of concerns about entering a nonpermissive environment and putting U.S. troops in harm's way. These are legitimate concerns, but under the International Security Assistance Force in Afghanistan, the Joint Incident Assessment Team regularly visited sites of alleged civilian harm to collect additional evidence to inform assessments, showing that such a practice can be feasible in at least some contexts if it is resourced and prioritized. In some cases, the U.S. military might make the decision that a site visit is not a priority. However, if that choice is made, then leaders need to think about alternatives to offset the weaknesses of military sources of information. DoD should consider requiring the military to document the reasons why a site visit could not or should not be conducted during the assessment process.

Develop and Deploy a Tool or Data Environment to Improve Collection of, Access to, and Storage of Operational Data Related to Civilian Harm

Without reliable operational data and effective knowledge management on civilian casualty incidents, it will be more difficult for the military to understand the root causes of civilian casualties, characterize patterns of harm, and identify measures that U.S. forces can take to mitigate civilian harm while preserving mission-effectiveness and force protection. The U.S. military must improve its data collection and storage methods in order to draw upon accurate, up-to-date information when conducting civilian casualty assessments and other analyses. Improved records of and access to operational data will serve several stakeholder communities. Focusing on mission first, improved data collection and knowledge management will improve the military's ability to go beyond simply tracking incidents and will instead provide valuable trend analysis and research in support of improved military planning and mission-effectiveness. The ability to track civilian casualties should be considered analogous to monitoring such other operational data as the number of friendly force casualties and the number of enemy forces captured or killed.[5] Second, at the strategic level, improved data collection will enhance the situational awareness of DoD senior leaders, helping them make better strategic decisions and have more-productive and more-effective discussions with Congress, NGOs, and the public. Data-driven analysis provides the confidence and context that may influence the political decisions on appropriate warfighting policy. Data collection and storage will also improve lessons learned, professional military education, and joint and combined training activities by helping the joint force incorporate real-world best practices into its warfighting preparations. Finally, better data collection and storage will improve the military's ability to provide accurate information to affected civilians.

Given the fast pace, complex organizational structures, and frequent personnel turnover that come with joint and combined military operations, DoD needs a tool

---

[5] Lewis, 2013.

or data environment to track and store the on-hand data needed for civilian casualty assessments. One illustrative example of such a joint tool integrated with an operational command and control center is at SOCOM. The command developed its own, in-house system for tracking information related to possible civilian casualties. This tool collects comprehensive information on SOF strikes and integrates it into a single platform. Each strike or assault mission is linked to information about what was known before the strike (such as the associated intelligence development, collateral damage estimation, or derogatory information on the target); information about the operation itself (such as the location, date, time, type of weapon, fuzing, or on-scene commander mission report); and post-operation information, which could include both classified and open-source information (such as the combat assessment, intelligence reflections, related social media posts, NGO allegations of civilian casualties, and strike reporting from DoD Public Affairs).[6] The principal benefit of this system is that all information related to potential civilian casualties is available in one, accessible, easily searchable location that allows SOCOM to more quickly and accurately respond to reports of civilian casualties.

Although DoD officials have discussed the need for a similar tool that would consolidate strike log and civilian casualty data to enable more-accurate tracking and recording of incidents,[7] resources and staffing solutions have yet to be allocated, despite the fact that issues with DoD's civilian casualty records and systems have been widely understood since the first dedicated studies on DoD and civilian casualties a decade ago.[8] We recommend that the Secretary of Defense assign an office of primary responsibility to develop and deploy such a tool or data environment that would provide greater consolidation and increased integration of this information. Access to and integration of the data from multiple sources will likely be a significant challenge. The SOCOM system is a potential model, although it will be difficult to scale up such a system—which would require the capability to integrate information from every U.S. military unit—for large-scale combat operations.

---

[6] DoD official, interview with the authors, January 2021.

[7] A report on the resources needed to implement DoD's civilian casualty policy notes,

> The Department may require IT [information technology] equipment and support, possibly contracted, to develop and test software; to procure and install hardware in multiple locations; to perform system maintenance, and to provide data storage, in order to . . . ensure that accurate data regarding lethal effects, including kinetic strikes, conducted by U.S. military forces is recorded and maintained. (DoD, *Report on Resources to Implement the Civilian Casualty Policy of the Department of Defense*, Washington, D.C., January 23, 2020a, p. 6)

[8] Congress has also indicated that DoD should develop such a system. For example, in Section 1077 of the FY 2021 NDAA, Congress required DoD to provide a report on the resources needed for civilian casualty issues, including an estimate of the costs of "any specialized information technology equipment, support and maintenance, and data storage capabilities . . . to receive allegations of, assess, investigate, account for, and respond to allegations of civilian casualties resulting from United States military operations" (Public Law 116-283, William M. (Mac) Thornberry National Defense Authorization Act for Fiscal Year 2021, January 1, 2021).

Incorporate Civilian Harm into Pre-Operation Intelligence Estimates and Post-Operation Assessments of the Cumulative Effect of Targeting Decisions

Most intelligence efforts in support of mitigating civilian harm are conducted in the planning stages of an operation or strike, and military doctrine and manuals reflect this focus. Post-operation damage assessments conducted by intelligence analysts are placed in the context of whether the military objective was achieved or the weaponeering choice was effective, not in the context of supporting assessments on the status of civilians who inhabit the area. Although the March 2019 revision of CJCSI 3162.02 now requires, rather than recommends, a combat assessment for target engagements, collateral damage assessments are conducted when the battle damage assessment notes that collateral damage occurred.[9] As noted previously, self-reporting of potential civilian harm is difficult—and nearly impossible if U.S. forces were unaware of civilians hidden inside of structures. Therefore, if civilians are not identified before or immediately after a strike, it is likely that U.S. forces will not conduct a collateral damage assessment unless someone witnesses physical damage to a nontargeted building. Moreover, doctrine and training do not focus on assessing a military operation's holistic impact on the civilian population or how to focus follow-on collection and assessment of civilian casualty reports.

We thus have three suggestions within this overall recommendation. First, we recommend that DoD incorporate civilian protection into network assessments of the cumulative effect of targeting decisions and campaigns. This holistic network assessment can leverage the current battle damage assessment analysis process,[10] but instead of focusing on the impact that strikes had on enemy networks, the assessment should consider factors relating to how civilians live and move within the environment. Second, to complement this effort, we recommend that the defense intelligence enterprise, particularly the Defense Intelligence Agency and NGA, develop analytic tradecraft and methodologies to identify best practices to validate, incorporate, and analyze open-source data related to human terrain, activity, and movements within an area of active operations to support intelligence preparation of the battlespace and civilian casualty assessments. Finally, we recommend that the intelligence analysts continue efforts to collect open-source information and fuse it with operational data (including ISR and FMV feeds and tactical data) to feed into running estimates during operations. In addition to building tools, DoD will likely need to develop analytic tradecraft and methodologies.

---

[9] CJCSI 3162.02, 2019.

[10] CJCSI 3162.02, 2019; and Joint Targeting School, "Joint Targeting School Student Guide," Dam Neck, Va., March 1, 2017.

Use a Range of Estimates of Civilian Casualties to Improve the Quality of Assessments

As detailed in Chapter Two of this report, the decisionmaking criteria in the military's assessment process can result in a systemic undercounting of civilian casualties for some scenarios, especially those involving strikes on structures. In our analysis of the military's assessments, the standard for credible incidents of civilian casualties often required that military sources showed positive proof indicating civilian harm. Thus, our fourth recommendation focuses on gaining a more accurate and holistic understanding of actual civilian casualty numbers and dealing with the inherent uncertainty involved with generating estimates. One way to do this is to adopt the recommendation in the 2018 Joint Staff review to use a range of estimates of civilian harm, with the minimum being the number that can be confirmed with military information and the maximum being the number that can be neither confirmed nor denied by military information. This step would improve civilian casualty estimates by avoiding the use of a standard of finding incidents credible that is higher than advertised. Such a step would help DoD be more consistent with its assessment standard for finding incidents credible and would help address the systemic underreporting for some contexts. In addition, given DoD concerns about tracking civilian harm in high-intensity conflicts, using a range of civilian-harm estimates would help address the inherent uncertainty that could arise in a high-intensity and geographically widespread conflict.

Establish Guidance on the Responsibilities of U.S. Military Forces in Monitoring Partners' Conduct and Offer Assistance to Partners in Building Their Own Assessment Capabilities If Needed

As we have noted in this report, the United States does not typically track instances of civilian harm caused by its partner forces. As described in our companion report,

> This can lead to an accountability gap because harm caused by local forces—who might be armed, trained, or supported by the United States—cannot be identified or mitigated. Understanding how U.S. partners are using U.S.-supplied weapons, training, and support is critical to informed policymaking. DoD, in coordination with other U.S. government agencies, should establish clear guidance on the responsibilities of U.S. military forces and other U.S. personnel in monitoring the conduct of partners. Where feasible, the military should consider establishing a process for gathering information on partner units and civilian harm, including how assistance is being used by partners in combat operations.[11]

The U.S. government could leverage three sources of information for this "operational end-use monitoring."[12] First, partners themselves might provide information—

---

[11] McNerney et al., forthcoming, p. 100.

[12] Lewis, 2019b, p. iii.

for example, on the location of the strikes, the type of weapon used, or the intended target. However, access is not guaranteed, and many partners may be reluctant to share data with the United States because such information is often very sensitive or classified. Nevertheless, there is precedent for partners sharing this type of data. For example, the Saudi-led coalition in Yemen documented basic details on every strike conducted in the campaign, and this information was sometimes made available when the United States specifically requested it—although the level of detail was often quite thin.[13] Second, DoD can leverage U.S. government information that could provide a better understand of what partners are doing on the ground. For example, after-action reports from exercises or reporting from embassies provide valuable information on partners' strengths and weaknesses and could be used to inform U.S. awareness of potential civilian harm–related issues and possible areas for future engagement. Collecting more-specific information on partner-caused civilian casualties would involve establishing (and prioritizing) new requirements—an idea that might receive pushback, given the ever-expanding number of requirements and the importance of focusing on threats from adversaries. In some instances, though, various parts of the U.S. government might already be collecting relevant information for other purposes that might help answer questions related to civilian harm. This is a sensitive topic but could be considered on a case-by-case basis for partners of concern. Finally, DoD could leverage open-source information, such as that from civil society organizations and social media.

Where this type of monitoring is not feasible, DoD should urge partners to conduct their own assessments of civilian harm. If partners lack the capacity to do this, U.S. forces should offer assistance in developing mechanisms for monitoring and assessments. Where appropriate, the development and implementation of such mechanisms could be a requirement of future assistance or support.

Expand Guidance on Civilian-Harm Assessments Across the Full Spectrum of Armed Conflict

We found that assessments might be challenging in high-intensity conflicts. Thus, our fifth recommendation focuses on how civilian assessments should be conducted during high-end conflict, including against near-peer adversaries.

DoD will need to consider how policies and procedures for assessments of civilian harm can be adjusted and scaled to account for the types of contingencies that might arise in theaters outside of CENTCOM and AFRICOM. Currently, many U.S. military officials in EUCOM and INDOPACOM are hard-pressed to see how they can apply existing assessment policies to potential armed conflict scenarios in their AORs. They will be better prepared to respond to potential civilian-harm incidents if guidance explicitly addresses assessments in scenarios beyond low- and medium-intensity

---

[13] Lewis, 2019b, p. 29; DoD official, interview with the authors, January 2021.

conflict. In particular, revised guidance should stress that noncombatants are a perma-nent feature of conflict, and civilians will retain agency in terms of their decisions to fight, flee, or remain. Training and planning scenarios in which civilians are conspicu-ously absent under the assumption that they have already evacuated are an incomplete representation of reality. To address this gap, DoD guidance should stipulate that all combatant commands incorporate civilian-harm assessment efforts into their opera-tional and contingency plans, including their intelligence requirements.

Recommendations for Investigations of Civilian Harm

Implement a Standardized Civilian-Harm Operational Reporting Process Intended to Support Learning

This report makes clear that current U.S. military investigations and reporting pro-cesses are not adequate for the U.S. military to take a learning approach to monitoring and responding to civilian harm. One solution to address this gap is to set a standard requirement for investigations of civilian harm, both to improve the ability to learn from individual incidents and to establish a process to systematically extract data that can be more easily disseminated and analyzed for the purpose of learning collectively from incidents. This solution, however, still carries the resource-intense burden of such investigations, as well as the stigma of wrongdoing that investigations tend to have.

Alternatively, DoD might develop a new reporting process specifically for the purpose of learning. This process could take several approaches, which vary in the level of resources needed. For example, one option is the safety investigation approach: The commercial airline community developed safety and accident board investigations to identify safety risks and lessons learned in nonpunitive environments. Individuals who provide information in the context of such investigations are offered protection from legal or disciplinary action; the goal is to obtain the most-complete and most-accurate picture of what happened and why to promote learning.[14] Although this would likely be an effective approach to improving the civilian casualty investigations process, the safety investigation process shares the resource-intensive nature of commander-directed investigations and is thus likely not a practical solution for larger-scale opera-tions involving hundreds of civilian-harm incidents, as we saw in OIR. It would also not be appropriate to use such investigations to cover up war crimes or other inten-tional violations of the law of war.

One of the challenges of learning from civilian casualty incidents is the uneven level of detail provided about an incident, a problem seen in both investigations and CCARs. One way to improve the consistency and availability of critical details is to standardize initial operational reporting of confirmed or suspected incidents of civil-

---

[14] Sewall and Lewis, 2010.

ian harm. Such a process was used under the International Security Assistance Force in Afghanistan, and the output there was called an initial impressions report. We suggest a similar process for U.S. operations overall in which units involved in confirmed or suspected civilian harm create a concise report containing essential facts that are easily accessible to operational forces, preferably within 24 hours. Although the initial impressions report in Afghanistan was structured to support initial public affairs efforts at higher headquarters, we propose a modified version that supports operational learning. At a minimum, such a report would include the following details:

- date and time of incident, including whether it was day or night
- location of incident (with coordinates)
- reporting unit and point of contact, plus responsible unit (if different)
- type of operation (e.g., air strike, artillery) and context (deliberate, dynamic, self-defense)
- operational narrative (a description of what happened, with the facts and circumstances that led to civilian harm)
- shooter location (coordinates and description) and location of intended target (coordinates and description)
- documentation of the combat assessment or battle damage assessment and other evidence regarding the effects of the engagement
- estimate of the civilian harm (number killed and wounded, including a range of numbers if necessary), with details (e.g., name, age or adult/child, gender, type of injury) as available
- weapon system and ammunition (with number of rounds) used and the platform from which the weapon was used
- how the target was identified as hostile
- whether the civilian harm resulted from a misidentification or was caused by collateral effects of the engagement
- whether civilian harm was estimated or anticipated from the engagement
- whether the location of the strike causing civilian harm was on the no-strike list or restricted target list or was near such an entity
- whether there was effective enemy fire during the engagement
- whether there was any obscuration of the target
- whether there was a weapon malfunction
- consequence-management steps taken, if any (e.g., medical care, meeting with victims or others, condolence payments, public affairs statements), including an assessment of the effectiveness of the response.

Instead of relying on a resource-intensive investigation process, the military could use this strengthened initial reporting process to preserve essential details that can be used, along with CCARs, for analyzing why individual incidents occurred and what steps could be taken to help avoid them. The data can also be used to understand the larger context, what factors tend to contribute more to civilian harm, and the trends and root causes of incidents to help inform steps that can be taken to reduce civilian harm. In addition, the data can inform which U.S. responses to civilian-harm incidents are most effective or well received. For example, because these initial reports would include descriptions of all responses taken by U.S. forces to provide assistance to affected civilians (including the provision of *ex gratia* payments), the military could better characterize whether civilians responded positively or negatively to U.S. offers of assistance and identify favorable practices that could then inform future response efforts. These initial reports can also be used to inform initial public affairs strategies regarding suspected civilian-harm incidents.

In sum, strengthening initial operational reporting as we have described here would give a stronger foundation for effective learning while avoiding the resource-intensive commitment of commander-directed investigations. Overall, for DoD to effectively learn and improve its ability to reduce civilian harm, it needs to either improve current investigation processes with learning in mind or create new processes that contain a specific mandate to promote learning about civilian-harm incidents.

Recommendations for Responses to Civilian Harm

In DoD Guidance, Avoid Placing Overly Restrictive Limits on Why, Where, and to Whom the U.S. Military Distributes Condolence Payments

Our research suggests that Section 1213 of the FY 2020 NDAA and DoD's June 2020 interim regulations on *ex gratia* payments place too many limits on the application of payments. As detailed in Chapter Four, the interim regulations note that the principal goal of *ex gratia* payments is to "maintain friendly relations with and the support of local populations where U.S. forces are operating" and may be provided only to "friendly civilians."[15] The singular focus on *ex gratia* payment as a strategic tool makes it difficult for commanders and operators outside of CENTCOM and AFRICOM, where the overwhelming majority of COIN and counterterrorism operations have taken place, to see the value and ultimately the feasibility of implementing such policies in other AORs. Indeed, our conversations with U.S. military personnel in INDOPACOM and EUCOM, as well as with former U.S. military legal personnel, suggest that, unless the guidance portrays the provision of condolences as a part of the U.S. military's process for responding to civilian harm across the full spectrum of conflict, any new regulation is unlikely to be enduring. Some combatant commands do not know how they would respond to incidents of unintended harm during high-intensity conflict against a near-peer adversary.

---

[15] U.S. Under Secretary of Defense for Policy, 2020, pp. 1, 4.

DoD guidance around responses to civilian harm should not make explicit or implicit exceptions; all U.S. military forces, regardless of geographic location and conflict type, will need to respond to civilian harm. At a minimum, this should be clear in a revised regulation on *ex gratia* payments. We recommend that DoD reframe its revised guidance to make *ex gratia* payments applicable beyond the COIN and stability operation context on which it currently appears to center. To do this, Congress would likely need to alter the language of Section 1213. Specifically, DoD's final guidance should be couched in language that emphasizes condolences as a humanitarian tool and should outline the strategic purposes that condolences can serve in maintaining the support of local populations. Moreover, the new policy could also focus more on how combatant commands are preparing for contingencies; for example, the policy could specify that the commands incorporate a civilian casualty response element into planning for future conflict.

In DoD's Final Policy on *Ex Gratia* Payments, Include Additional Transparency Around How Payment Amounts Are Determined and How the Payments Are Disbursed

Although the June 2020 interim regulations include important improvements to DoD's policy for responding to civilian casualty events, there is still room to increase DoD's transparency about policy specifics. In particular, the final policy should require commanders to provide additional details about *ex gratia* payments, such as the location of payments, circumstances under which they were made, and the number of individuals across which payments were divided. As currently written, the regulation allows for an inconsistent application of condolences to harmed civilians and does not allay concerns around the wide discrepancies that exist across payment amounts. Additional transparency requirements in this regard would help avoid the disbursement of widely divergent *ex gratia* payments and improve the military's ability to assess the effectiveness of payments and identify best practices to inform future response efforts.

Moreover, although current guidance specifies that combatant commands must publicly release information about *ex gratia* payments made to civilians, it does not mandate reporting on offers that were made but refused by civilians. By also releasing data on offers that were subsequently refused by survivors of civilian harm, DoD will further increase transparency around its condolence policy and provide an additional mechanism to learn from past experiences.

Finally, future DoD guidance should be more clear in specifying mechanisms and processes through which victims of harm can make claims and receive condolences.

Provide Guidance and Training on All Options Available to Commanders to Respond to Civilian Harm

DoD guidance on responses to civilian harm should be more comprehensive and address a fuller suite of response options (in addition to monetary condolences) that

U.S. military commanders have at their disposal after a civilian-harm event. One approach is to develop locally grounded responses that take into account the unique needs of individual victims. For instance, additional guidance could outline a variety of responses in addition to *ex gratia* payments, such as basic acknowledgment of harm and community contributions. Appropriate responses should be decided on a case-by-case basis and should draw on interaction and engagement with victims. In one of our interviews, a representative of a civil society organization stressed that "understanding what [victims] would like to see would be a dignified gesture,"[16] and operators with combat experience in Iraq and Afghanistan have stressed that interacting directly with local populations helps build trust and respect for U.S. forces.[17] In short, locally informed responses provide tangible evidence to victims and the public more broadly that U.S. forces take reports of potential civilian harm seriously and are willing to fully engage in a robust and inclusive investigation and response process.

Finally, DoD does not have training for U.S. military personnel charged with responding to civilian casualties, including making *ex gratia* payments. For DoD policy on civilian-harm response to be meaningful and consistently applied across U.S. military forces, DoD should mandate that training on the policy be delivered to legal staff, as well as commanders and operators who will use it in active combat operations.

Recommendations Regarding DoD Resourcing and Structure to Address Civilian Harm

Create Dedicated, Permanent Positions for Protection of Civilians in Each Geographic Combatant Command and Across DoD, and Establish Working Groups of Rotating Personnel for Additional Support

DoD should improve its resourcing and structure to address weaknesses in pre- and post-strike civilian casualty processes. Some of these weaknesses arise from a significant shortage of permanent personnel dedicated to civilian-harm issues. As we have documented in this report, personnel in CENTCOM and AFRICOM are often assigned to civilian-harm issues as collateral duties, while EUCOM, INDOPACOM, and SOUTHCOM do not have any dedicated personnel or established CIVCAS cells. Although EUCOM, INDOPACOM, and SOUTHCOM are not engaged in warfighting operations at this time, EUCOM and INDOPACOM are regularly planning for future hostilities and maintain fires billets for such purposes. And all three commands are engaged in activities that fall under the broader mandate of civilian

---

[16] Civil society organization representative, interview with the authors, June 2020.

[17] Current and former military operators, interview with the authors, May 2020.

protection.[18] For example, they support partner military forces in military operations, work to prevent human rights violations, support efforts to counter human trafficking, promote the role of women in peace and security issues, and promote adherence to law of war principles. In addition, these commands will have the responsibility to mitigate, assess, and respond to civilian casualty incidents in potential future conflicts, which is a particularly daunting planning challenge for EUCOM and INDOPACOM.

Congress included a provision (Section 923) in the FY 2020 NDAA requiring DoD to submit a report assessing the resources it needed to meet its requirements for civilian-harm mitigation and response in practice.[19] This report might have been an opportunity for DoD to provide a detailed accounting of the personnel and resources it needed. However, beyond noting that DoD "may require additional personnel" in the near term at OSD, the Joint Staff, and the GCCs, the report provided little additional specificity.[20] In the FY 2021 NDAA, Congress again required DoD to provide a report on civilian casualty resourcing and specifically requested an "estimate of the number of personnel" required over the next three years.[21] In a separate section of the same NDAA, Congress encouraged DoD "to make additional progress in ensuring that the combatant commands have the requisite personnel and resources" to integrate civilian protection in the commands' planning and activities.[22] This is an institutional responsibility that OSD, the Joint Staff, and the military services need to address. In this section, we present some broad suggestions for how DoD might resource and structure itself to meet its civilian protection responsibilities. We also recommend that DoD conduct an official manpower study in order to determine long-term staffing and structural changes tailored to each relevant DoD component. Such a study should also include a review of what resources the military services need to effectively organize, train, and equip U.S. military forces to address the full variety of civilian-harm issues that they face during operations. The study should also review manpower requirements to support training of GCC and other DoD component staff.

During our interviews, many DoD and NGO personnel expressed their desire to see CIVCAS cells in all GCCs and at relevant subordinate operational commands resourced with permanent personnel as a way of improving U.S. military assessments, investigations, and responses to civilian harm. However, the diversity of missions and objectives across combatant commands suggests that any permanent position should

---

[18] According to Army Techniques Publication 3-07.6, "Protection of civilians refers to efforts that reduce civilian risks from physical violence, secure their rights to access essential services and resources, and contribute to a secure, stable, and just environment for civilians over the long-term" (Army Techniques Publication 3-07.6, 2015, p. 1-1).

[19] Pub. L. 116-92, 2019; for the resulting report, see DoD, 2020a.

[20] DoD, 2020a.

[21] Pub. L. 116-283, 2021.

[22] Pub. L. 116-283, 2021.

be flexible enough to address the unique needs that arise across regions. In this vein, we recommend that future DoD guidance instruct all GCCs to develop more-robust structures focused on the broader mandate of protecting civilians—including addressing civilian-harm issues. As a starting point, DoD would staff these civilian protection offices with at least four permanent personnel, plus additional personnel as required to support initiatives that may prove more labor-intensive for particular GCCs (e.g., SOUTHCOM's human rights promotion efforts or GCCs with robust programs for promoting the role of women in peace and security).

Our analysis of current GCC operations—which are admittedly quite diverse—led us to estimate that four people would provide a strong foundation with sufficient bandwidth to more proactively play several roles, depending on their situation. Related tasks would include the following:

- Oversee civilian-harm assessments, investigations, and responses.
- Analyze data on civilian casualty trends.
- Identify training and equipment requirements, including to the military services.
- Improve the incorporation of civilian-harm considerations into fires cells and operational planning teams.
- Support public affairs offices and engage NGOs.
- Develop simulations, workshops, and exercises that stress-test various conflict scenarios from a civilian-harm perspective.
- Advance other programs relevant to civilian protection, such as human rights, women's role in peace and security, and mass-atrocity response operations.

Four personnel is an estimate based on our research, so we recommend that exact staffing levels be analyzed and reassessed as part of the DoD-wide manpower study recommended earlier in this section.

Each GCC should tailor its civilian protection office and its associated personnel positions to fit the needs of the AOR. SOUTHCOM, for example, could take a more comprehensive approach to civilian protection issues while continuing its primary focus on human rights. INDOPACOM and EUCOM might focus on improving planning and collaboration with allies and partners on civilian protection issues, including efforts to mitigate civilian-harm risks in high-intensity combat. In addition to enhancing their ongoing civilian-harm assessments, investigations, and responses, CENTCOM and AFRICOM could leverage these personnel to better integrate civilian protection considerations into advise, assist, and accompany missions with partner military forces.

These new civilian protection positions should be filled by civilians with relevant expertise, who would receive support from rotating military personnel with expertise in the operations, planning, legal, public affairs, intelligence, and other relevant military occupational specialties. For example, other billets that would be relevant to improving the U.S. military's response to civilian-harm incidents could include operators from the ground or air communities with relevant combat experience. Additionally, military analysts with skills in such areas as operations research and systems analysis could leverage their expertise in statistical modeling and simulation tools to provide analysis on civilian casualties and civilian protection more broadly and develop training packages across the commands.

The CIVCAS cells, which we recommend be established for the GCCs and subordinate commands overseeing named U.S. military operations, would reside organizationally under the GCCs' civilian protection offices, but individual staff should be embedded within the commands' military operations and planning directorates. In addition to improving planning and operations, assessments of civilian casualties are more effective and less vulnerable to politicization when done in close coordination with military operators.[23] Moreover, such a structure can help engender trust between operators and planners and the personnel assigned to the cell. We recommend that each CIVCAS cell be led by a civilian (possibly a retired military officer with relevant operational experience) who can preserve institutional knowledge and oversee a team of mostly military officers who can work effectively at the intersections of military, intelligence, and NGO communities. Despite the critical role of intelligence in operational planning, targeting, and damage assessments,[24] the extent to which it is formally integrated into combatant command and component CIVCAS cells varies. AFRICOM and CJTF-OIR civilian casualty cells deliberately include a member with an intelligence background, while CENTCOM and RS personnel consult intelligence only as required on a case-by-case basis.[25] Formally including intelligence efforts with operations, legal, and public affairs expertise would ensure that all required competencies are represented upon first receipt of civilian casualty reports. We recommend a permanent position in each CIVCAS cell for an intelligence analyst who has been trained in leveraging intelligence sources, and who will search for new information following operations, to support civilian casualty assessments. EUCOM and INDOPACOM should have plans to rapidly scale up a CIVCAS cell of a similar structure if the United States becomes involved in a military conflict in their respective regions.

Finally, given the potential DoD-wide impact of more-strategic, analysis-based proactive attention to these issues, we recommend that additional permanent positions be established in several offices in the Pentagon. We recommend that a second permanent billet be established within OSD's policy division and that half- to full-time

---

[23] NGO official, interview with the authors, December 2020.

[24] See, for example, Joint Publication 2-01, 2017; Joint Publication 3-60, 2018; and CJCSI 3162.02, 2019.

[25] AFRICOM official, interview with the authors, April 2020, May 2020; CENTCOM and CJTF-OIR officials, interview with the authors, June 2020; CENTCOM and CJTF-OIR officials, interview with the authors, June 2020; CENTCOM military official, email correspondence with the authors, June 2020; RS officials, interview with the authors, May 2020.

billets be assigned to OSD's intelligence, research and engineering, acquisition and sustainment, and personnel and readiness divisions. Each of these OSD organizations could play a more proactive role in improving DoD's civilian casualty policies and procedures in their respective areas, such as intelligence, technology and acquisition (including data management), and training.

We also recommend that the Joint Staff add an additional full-time billet so the organization can take a more active role with the military services in such areas as doctrine, data analysis, lessons learned, training, and professional military education. Again, these recommendations are based on our initial research that should be reviewed more thoroughly in a DoD-wide manpower study.

Create a Center of Excellence for Civilian Protection

The additional manpower resources that we outlined in the previous recommendation would establish a stronger foundation for DoD's civilian protection efforts. These improvements would create an even greater demand, however, for an organizational hub or nexus for expertise, energy, and DoD-wide collaboration. Although OSD and the Joint Staff serve important oversight and coordination functions, these organizations will always remain focused on high-level policies and procedures in support of the Secretary of Defense and the Chairman of the Joint Chiefs of Staff, respectively. As more people in DoD become involved in civilian protection, requirements will grow for experts who can support such tasks as data collection and analysis, the development and dissemination of lessons learned, and the facilitation of collaboration. The effective promotion of civilian protection requires a diverse mix of expertise in such areas as conflict management, humanitarian crisis response, law of war, NGO engagement, information management, intelligence, military planning and operations, training, professional military education, and research and analysis. Although the military services will be able to develop and provide some of this expertise, an organization with a strong civil-military culture that can work across DoD would serve a crucial supporting role and as a catalyst, allowing the whole of DoD's efforts to become far greater than the sum of its wide-ranging parts. Thus, we recommend that OSD and the Joint Staff, working closely with the military services and GCCs, create a civilian protection center of excellence to coordinate and conduct research, analytic and operational support, education and training, and dissemination of lessons learned. Center staff would also be a source of support by providing reach-back services, deployable experts, and institutional knowledge management and by serving as a catalyst for collaboration among stakeholders within DoD, the wider U.S. government, the NGO community, and the international community. The center could host an annual lessons-learned conference and issue an annual report that leverages past civilian casualty assessments to improve DoD-wide and international learning. During periods of conflict when civilian casualty incidents are high, these activities could be more frequent.

We recommend starting with at least a handful of staff with a mix of civilians and military personnel and experience in the areas described earlier in this section. As the center establishes itself as a hub for civilian-harm assessments and learning, it could expand its mandate into the broader variety of protection issues described earlier. DoD might look to several existing centers for ideas about organizational structure, staffing, funding, and operations. The Joint Staff oversees "chairman-controlled activities"—for example, the Joint Center for International Security Force Assistance, which institutionalizes security force assistance doctrine, tactics, techniques, and procedures across DoD. Another example is DoD's Joint Enabling Capabilities Command, which can provide GCCs and JTFs with capabilities and experts in joint planning, communications, and public affairs. The Army's Peacekeeping and Stability Operations Institute serves as DoD's "lead agent for joint proponency for peace and stability operations."[26] An internationally focused example of existing centers is the Defense Institute of International Legal Studies, which is the lead DoD security cooperation resource for global legal engagement and capacity-building with international defense sector officials. Although none of these examples provides a perfect template, they do illustrate useful precedents.

Maintain the Capability to Conduct Periodic Reviews to Monitor Civilian-Harm Trends over Time and Address Emerging Issues

DoD should establish a policy of conducting periodic operational reviews to monitor civilian casualty trends and patterns over time in order to help identify emerging issues and address them in a timely way.[27] This would be similar to the approach DoD took in Afghanistan from 2009 to 2012. The Office of the Under Secretary of Defense for Policy could start this process by directing an operational review for Afghanistan. Because the North Atlantic Treaty Organization's RS headquarters did not provide requested data within the timeline of the 2018 Joint Staff review, Afghanistan was not included in that study. Such a review for Afghanistan operations not only would be justifiable to meet the intent of the Joint Staff review but also would be particularly timely in light of our analysis showing a recent and dramatic increase in civilian casualties. This reported increase coincides with changes in guidance and in the tempo and nature of U.S. operations in Afghanistan. Such an operational review would help clarify actual risks to civilians, explain reasons for any discrepancies between U.S. and observer reporting, give the United States a foundation for better addressing risks to civilians in the current operating environment, and allow DoD to draw lessons to inform future military operations. After an initial review, should U.S. military efforts

---

[26] U.S. Army War College Foundation, "Peacekeeping and Stability Operations Institute (PKSOI)," webpage, undated.

[27] Larry Lewis, "Recommendations for Strengthening Civilian Protection," Arlington, Va.: CNA, unpublished working paper, October 2020.

in Afghanistan continue, this effort should be sustained by conducting reviews every six months. A similar periodic approach should be taken moving forward for other U.S. operations. These reviews could be led jointly by OSD and the Joint Staff, or they could be done independently by other DoD organizations or by federally funded research and development centers. The center of excellence described in the previous recommendation could conduct or support these reviews, once it is established.

When CIVCAS Cells Are Established at Joint Task Forces, Define Processes for Reverting Responsibilities and Data Back to the Command's Headquarters

In addition to developing consistent processes for establishing CIVCAS cells at GCCs and JTFs, GCCs should also determine specific guidelines and processes for reverting those responsibilities and data back to GCC headquarters when operations cease. Considering how to move data from a forward-deployed location and when authorities and responsibilities related to civilian casualty assessments should revert to GCC headquarters at the beginning of a new operation will ensure that this critical information and responsibility is not lost in the shuffle. Ultimately, GCCs are responsible for ensuring that such processes as data archival are effective. If they choose to delegate to subordinate operational commands, they must ensure that they get that information back and archive it properly when the operational command goes away.

Geographic Combatant Command Procedures for Civilian Casualty Assessments

The appendix to this report is available for download at www.rand.org/t/RRA418-1.

Abbreviations

AFRICOM	U.S. Africa Command
AOR	area of responsibility
AR	Army Regulation
CCAR	CIVCAS credibility assessment report
CCMT	Civilian Casualty Mitigation Team
CENTCOM	U.S. Central Command
CFE-DM	Center for Excellence in Disaster Management and Humanitarian Assistance
CIVCAS cell	civilian casualty cell
CJCSI	Chairman of the Joint Chiefs of Staff Instruction
CJTF	Combined Joint Task Force
COIN	counterinsurgency
DoD	U.S. Department of Defense
EUCOM	U.S. European Command
FMV	full-motion video
FY	fiscal year
GCC	geographic combatant command
INDOPACOM	U.S. Indo-Pacific Command
ISIS	Islamic State of Iraq and Syria
ISR	intelligence, surveillance, and reconnaissance
JTF	joint task force
NDAA	National Defense Authorization Act
NGA	National Geospatial-Intelligence Agency
NGO	nongovernmental organization
OIR	Operation Inherent Resolve

RS	Resolute Support
SOCOM	U.S. Special Operations Command
SOF	special operations forces
SOUTHCOM	U.S. Southern Command

References

Adams, Katharine M. E., "A Permanent Framework for Condolence Payments in Armed Conflict: A Vital Commander's Tool," *Military Law Review*, Vol. 224, No. 2, 2016, pp. 314–372.

Administrator of the Coalition Provisional Authority, "Commanders' Emergency Response Program," memorandum to the Commander of Coalition Forces, June 16, 2003.

Air Force Instruction 51-401, *The Law of War*, Department of the Air Force, August 3, 2018.

Airwars, "U.S.-Led Coalition in Iraq & Syria," webpage, undated. As of March 1, 2021:
https://airwars.org/conflict/coalition-in-iraq-and-syria/

———, "Civilian Casualties: Airwars Assessment," incident CS598, March 20, 2017. As of March 28, 2021:
https://airwars.org/civilian-casualties/cs598-march-20-2017/

——— [@airwars], "Recently we learned from @DeptofDefense that 611 ex gratia payments . . . ," Twitter post, June 24, 2020. As of March 28, 2021:
https://twitter.com/airwars/status/1275762907062644737

Amnesty International, "War in Raqqa: Rhetoric Versus Reality," webpage, undated. As of March 1, 2021:
https://raqqa.amnesty.org

———, *"I Won't Forget This Carnage": Civilians Trapped in Battle for Raqqa – Syria*, London, 2017.

Army Regulation 15-6, *Procedures for Administrative Investigations and Boards of Officers*, Washington, D.C.: Headquarters, Department of the Army, April 1, 2016.

Army Tactics, Techniques, and Procedures 3-37.31, *Civilian Casualty Mitigation*, Washington, D.C.: Headquarters, Department of the Army, July 2012.

Army Techniques Publication 3-07.6, *Protection of Civilians*, Headquarters, Department of the Army, October 29, 2015.

CENTCOM—*See* U.S. Central Command.

Center for Civilians in Conflict, "Ex-Gratia Payments in Afghanistan: A Case for Standing Policy for the US Military," issue brief, May 11, 2015.

Chairman of the Joint Chiefs of Staff Instruction 3160.01C, *No-Strike and Collateral Damage Estimation Methodology*, Washington, D.C.: Joint Chiefs of Staff, 2018, Not available to the general public.

Chairman of the Joint Chiefs of Staff Instruction 3162.02, *Methodology for Combat Assessment*, Washington, D.C.: Joint Chiefs of Staff, March 8, 2019.

Chairman of the Joint Chiefs of Staff Instruction 3370.01B, *Target Development Standards*, Washington, D.C.: Joint Chiefs of Staff, May 6, 2016, Not available to the general public.

Chief, J3, "RS/USFOR-A 2019 Civilian Casualty Allegation and Mitigation Information Paper," Kabul: Headquarters Resolute Support, January 30, 2020.

CJCSI—*See* Chairman of the Joint Chiefs of Staff Instruction.

CJTF-OIR—*See* Combined Joint Task Force – Operation Inherent Resolve.

Cohen, Raphael S., Nathan Chandler, Shira Efron, Bryan Frederick, Eugeniu Han, Kurt Klein, Forrest E. Morgan, Ashley L. Rhoades, Howard J. Shatz, and Yuliya Shokh, *The Future of Warfare in 2030: Project Overview and Conclusions*, Santa Monica, Calif.: RAND Corporation, RR-2849/1-AF, 2020. As of March 28, 2021:
https://www.rand.org/pubs/research_reports/RR2849z1.html

Combined Joint Task Force – Operation Inherent Resolve, "CIVCAS Releases," webpage, undated-a. As of March 28, 2021:
https://www.inherentresolve.mil/Releases/CIVCAS-Releases/

———, "Strike Releases," webpage, undated-b. As of March 1, 2021:
https://www.inherentresolve.mil/Releases/Strike-Releases/

———, *Combined Joint Task Force – Operation Inherent Resolve (CJTF-OIR) Policy for Reporting and Responding to Civilian Casualty Incidents*, Camp Arifjan, Kuwait, May 9, 2018a.

———, "CJTF-OIR Monthly Civilian Casualty Report," press release, June 28, 2018b.

DoD—*See* U.S. Department of Defense.

Executive Order 13732, "United States Policy on Pre- and Post-Strike Measures to Address Civilian Casualties in U.S. Operations Involving the Use of Force," White House, July 1, 2016.

Field Manual 6-0, *Commander and Staff Organization and Operations*, Washington, D.C.: Headquarters, Department of the Army, April 22, 2016.

Field Manual 6-27, *The Commander's Handbook on the Law of Land Warfare*, Washington, D.C.: Department of the Army and Department of the Navy, August 2019.

Foundation for Defense of Democracies and the Brookings Institution, "Economic Defeat of the Islamic State: Behind the Scenes of Operation Tidal Wave II," panel, May 10, 2019.

Gordon, Thomas J., IV, Adam Oler, Laurie Blank, and Jill Goldenziel, "Lawyers, Guns, and Twitter: Wargamig the Role of Law in War," *War on the Rocks*, February 2, 2021.

Human Rights Watch, "Syria: U.S. Coalition Should Address Civilian Harm," July 9, 2019.

Joint Center for Operational Analysis, *Adaptive Learning for Afghanistan: Final Recommendations*, Suffolk, Va.: U.S. Joint Forces Command, February 10, 2011, Not available to the general public.

Joint Doctrine Note 4/13, *Culture and the Human Terrain*, London: U.K. Ministry of Defence, September 2013.

Joint Publication 2-01, *Joint and National Intelligence Support to Military Operations*, Washington, D.C.: Joint Chiefs of Staff, July 5, 2017.

Joint Publication 2-01.3, *Joint Intelligence Preparation of the Operational Environment*, Washington, D.C.: Joint Chiefs of Staff, May 21, 2014.

Joint Publication 3-0, *Joint Operations*, Washington, D.C.: Joint Chiefs of Staff, October 22, 2018.

Joint Publication 3-60, *Joint Targeting*, Washington, D.C.: Joint Chiefs of Staff, September 28, 2018, Not available to the general public.

Joint Staff, *Civilian Casualty (CIVCAS) Review*, Washington, D.C., April 17, 2018. As of March 1, 2021:
https://www.jcs.mil/Portals/36/Documents/Civilian%20Casualty%20Review%20Report%20Redacted.pdf

Joint Targeting School, "Joint Targeting School Student Guide," Dam Neck, Va., March 1, 2017.

Keenan, Marla B., and Jonathan Tracy, *US Military Claims System for Civilians*, Washington, D.C.: Center for Civilians in Conflict, 2008.

Khalfaoui, Anna, Daniel Mahanty, Alex Moorehead, and Priyanka Motaparthy, *In Search of Answers: U.S. Military Investigations and Civilian Harm*, Washington, D.C.: Center for Civilians in Conflict and Columbia Law School Human Rights Institute, 2020.

Khan, Azmat, and Anand Gopal, "The Uncounted," *New York Times Magazine*, November 16, 2017.

Kipp, Jacob, Lester Grau, Karl Prinslow, and Don Smith, "The Human Terrain System: A CORDS for the 21st Century," *Military Review*, September–October 2006, pp. 8–15.

Kolenda, Christopher D., Rachel Reid, Chris Rogers, and Marte Retzius, *The Strategic Costs of Civilian Harm: Applying Lessons from Afghanistan to Current and Future Conflicts*, New York: Open Society Foundations, June 2016.

Lewis, Larry, *Reducing and Mitigating Civilian Casualties: Enduring Lessons*, Washington, D.C.: Joint and Coalitional Operational Analysis, April 12, 2013.

———, "We Need an Independent Review of Drone Strikes," *War on the Rocks*, May 6, 2015.

———, "Reflecting on the Civilian Casualty Executive Order: What Was Lost and What Can Now Be Gained," *Just Security*, March 12, 2019a.

———, *Promoting Civilian Protection During Security Assistance: Learning from Yemen*, Arlington, Va.: CNA, May 2019b.

———, "Recommendations for Strengthening Civilian Protection," Arlington, Va.: CNA, unpublished working paper, October 2020.

Liveuamap, "About," webpage, undated. As of January 14, 2021:
https://liveuamap.com/about

Mahanty, Daniel R., Jenny McAvoy, and Archibald S. Henry, *The U.S. Military and Post-Harm Amends Policy and Programs: Key Considerations and NGO Recommendations*, Washington, D.C.: Center for Civilians in Conflict, March 2019.

Martin, Joseph, Matthew Isler, and Jeff Davis, "Department of Defense News Briefing on the Findings of an Investigation into a March 17 Coalition Air Strike in West Mosul," transcript, U.S. Department of Defense, May 25, 2017.

McNerney, Michael J., Gabrielle Tarini, Nate Rosenblatt, Karen Sudkamp, Pauline Moore, Michelle Grisé, Benjamin J. Sacks, and Larry Lewis, *Understanding Civilian Harm in Raqqa and Its Implications for Future Conflicts*, Santa Monica, Calif.: RAND Corporation, RR-A753-1, forthcoming.

Native, "Aid & Development," webpage, undated. As of March 28, 2021:
https://www.native.io/industries/aid_and_development

Oak Ridge National Laboratory, "Population Density Tables," presentation, June 2020.

Office of the General Counsel, U.S. Department of Defense, *Department of Defense Law of War Manual*, Washington, D.C.: U.S. Department of Defense, December 2016.

Operation Resolute Support Civilian Casualty Mitigation Team, "RAND CIVCAS Study – RS Response as of 28 April," Microsoft Word document provided to the authors, April 2020.

Pickup, Sharon L., Carole F. Coffey, Kelly Baumgartner, Krislin Bolling, Alissa Czyz, K. N. Harms, Ronald La Due Lake, Marcus L. Oliver, and Jason Pogacnik, *Military Operations: The Department of Defense's Use of Solatia and Condolence Payments in Iraq and Afghanistan*, Washington, D.C.: U.S. Government Accountability Office, May 1, 2007.

Prasow, Andrea, "Civilian Casualties: A Case for U.S. Condolence Payments in Syria," *Just Security*, January 6, 2020.

Public Law 116-92, National Defense Authorization Act for Fiscal Year 2020, Section 1721, December 20, 2019.

Public Law 116-283, William M. (Mac) Thornberry National Defense Authorization Act for Fiscal Year 2021, January 1, 2021.

Reeves, Philip, "Survivors of Afghan Hospital Airstrike Dissatisfied with Compensation Plan," NPR, April 11, 2016.

Ryan, Missy, "U.S. Military Made $2 Million in Civilian Casualties Payments in Afghanistan in Recent Years," *Washington Post,* August 17, 2020.

Sealr, homepage, undated. As of March 28, 2021:
https://www.sealr.app

Sewall, Sarah B., *Chasing Success: Air Force Efforts to Reduce Civilian Harm*, Maxwell Air Force Base, Ala.: Air Force University Press, 2016.

Sewall, Sarah, and Larry Lewis, *Reducing and Mitigating Civilian Casualties: Afghanistan and Beyond—Joint Civilian Casualty Study*, Washington, D.C.: Joint Center for Operational Analysis and U.S. Joint Forces Command, 2010, Not available to the general public.

Solvang, Ole, and Nadim Houry, *All Feasible Precautions? Civilian Casualties in Anti-ISIS Coalition Airstrikes in Syria*, New York: Human Rights Watch, September 24, 2017.

United Nations, *Report on the Independent International Commission of Inquiry on the Syrian Arab Republic*, New York, A/HRC/37/72, February 1, 2018.

United Nations Assistance Mission in Afghanistan, *Afghanistan: Protection of Civilians in Armed Conflict 2019*, Kabul, February 2020a.

———, *Afghanistan: Protection of Civilians in Armed Conflict—First Quarter Report: 1 January– 31 March 2020*, Kabul, April 2020b.

U.S. Africa Command Public Affairs, "AFRICOM Civilian Casualty Status Report Initiative," press release, March 31, 2020.

U.S. Army War College Foundation, "Peacekeeping and Stability Operations Institute (PKSOI)," webpage, undated. As of April 7, 2021:
https://usawc.org/peacekeeping-stability-operations-institute-pksoi-2/

U.S. Central Command, "March 21: Military Airstrikes Continue Against ISIS Terrorists in Syria and Iraq," press release, No. 17-112, March 21, 2017.

———, "RAND Study Responses JFE," Microsoft Word document with responses to author questions, May 2020.

U.S. Code, Title 10, Section 2734, Property Loss; Personal Injury or Death: Incident to Noncombat Activities of the Armed Forces; Foreign Countries.

U.S. Department of Defense, *Summary of the 2018 National Defense Strategy of the United States of America: Sharpening the American Military's Competitive Edge*, Washington, D.C., 2018a.

———, *Department of Defense Report on Civilian Casualties in Connection with United States Military Operations in 2017*, Washington, D.C., May 22, 2018b.

———, *Department of Defense Report on Civilian Casualties in Connection with United States Military Operations in 2018*, Washington, D.C., April 29, 2019.

———, *Report on Resources to Implement the Civilian Casualty Policy of the Department of Defense*, Washington, D.C., January 23, 2020a.

———, *Annual Report on Civilian Casualties in Connection with United States Military Operations in 2019*, Washington, D.C., April 22, 2020b.

U.S. Department of Defense Directive 2311.01E, *DoD Law of War Program*, Washington, D.C.: U.S. Department of Defense, November 15, 2010.

U.S. Forces Afghanistan, *Investigation Report of the Airstrike on the Médecins Sans Frontières/Doctors Without Borders Trauma Center in Kunduz, Afghanistan on 3 October 2015*, April 28, 2016.

———, "Memorandum for Record USFOR-A RAND Response," Microsoft Word document provided to the authors, USFOR-A-OPS-J5-CCMT, October 20, 2020.

U.S. Under Secretary of Defense for Policy, "Reporting Civilian Casualties," webpage, undated. As of March 28, 2021:
https://policy.defense.gov/OUSDP-Offices/Reporting-Civilian-Casualties/

———, "Interim Regulations for Condolence or Sympathy Payments to Friendly Civilians for Injury or Loss That Is Incident to Military Operations," memorandum for secretaries of the military departments, Chairman of the Joint Chiefs of Staff, and commanders of the combatant commands, June 22, 2020.